Legacy of
One-Room Schools

by

Myrna J. Grove

LEGACY OF ONE-ROOM SCHOOLS

Cover: *Collins School, located in Steuben County, Indiana, was built in 1877 as District No. 3 in Jamestown Township, and students were educated there until its closing in 1943. June Collins, current owner, is both a former student and a former teacher at the school. The school was originally platted on her Grandfather Collins' farm. Miss Collins organized restoration of the school in 1967. The maple trees surrounding the school were planted in 1900.*

Library of Congress Number: 99-75153
International Standard Book Number: 1-883294-92-4

Printed by
Masthof Press
220 Mill Road
Morgantown, PA 19543-9701

Prospect School was District No. 6 in Center Township, Williams County, Ohio.

Miss Stombaugh at Prospect School.

Dedication

I would like to dedicate this book to my mother, Florence Stombaugh Grove, who began her thirty-two-year teaching career in 1937 at one-room schools in Northwest Ohio. She taught at Prospect School and at Scott School, both in Williams County, after receiving a two-year Normal teaching degree from Manchester College in Indiana. Later, she completed further degrees and taught elementary grades at public schools in Pioneer and Edgerton, Ohio.

Contents

References in the text (example:
Gulliford 36) refer to the references
on pages 137-139.

This brick schoolhouse in Henry County, Ohio, on County Road 24 was built in 1894. It was most recently used as a grain storage building. The school typifies an abandoned brick country school.

*Do you have a little red schoolhouse
   safe in your memory,
With an iron stove and an outside pump
   and a shady maple tree?*

Helen Middleton

Introduction

Beside graveled back roads in the rural countryside, the casual traveler often passes by the abandoned remnants of a past era. In overgrown brush stands an isolated, rectangular building with sagging brick walls, broken-out windows, and a lopsided bell tower. Or, the traveler sees a gray, unpainted frame structure, covered with vines and open to the creatures of nature. Cornstalks and fields of wheat hug the darkened walls, and black iron pump handles rise above nearby quack grass. The decaying buildings give only a hint of their former use and importance.

For some travelers, the aging buildings bring back a rush of familiar and warmly-remembered images. But, younger persons can only imagine the crumbling structures as scenes of activity. Gone is the yard of green grass, the shrieks of children playing, the echo of bells clanging, and the bare spot marking home plate.

Sometimes, matching outhouses tilt off center in opposite corners of the

The Yellow Run School in Pulaski Township, Williams County, Ohio, was closed in 1936.

neglected lot. A few maple trees and fence posts border the edge of the acre. A narrow brook with stony banks lamely ripples by. A broken teeter-totter stands motionless, and a lean-to woodshed or coal house holds empty bins.

Inside the structures, missing frame glass windows allow birds to sit on the rafters. Coatless, wooden hooks hang crookedly near the front entrance. Grimy walls have been stripped bare except for the blackboard at the front. And grooves in the warped floorboards

Some former one-room schools have been left to decay. The school above is located in northern Indiana on Route 9 near Laud. Cows now graze around the privately-owned structure. Jackson School was open from 1891 to 1925.

This frame schoolhouse with its large entryway sits quietly by the roadside in western Michigan.

show where rows of wooden desks were once fastened to the floor.

What are these structures dotting the roadsides in a predictable pattern? Why does no one have the heart to tear them down and put them out of their misery?

Yes, some of them have been cleverly recycled. They now appear camouflaged as storage sheds, grange halls, craft shops, and small houses. But, often, their second use has also been abandoned, and the remodeled buildings are again left hauntingly silent.

This brick school in Lenawee County, Michigan, is now used as a craft shop. It is in close proximity to U.S. Route 12—better known as the Chicago Pike.

Another brick school in Lenawee County, Michigan, is now used as a craft shop.
It also is close to U.S. Route 12.

Chapter 1

The Northwest Territory
Surveys Shape Both Land and Society

One-room schoolhouses were a part of American history and social order for more than 350 years. Begun in New England, they were first suggested by the Court of Massachusetts in 1647 (Gulliford 36). The main purpose of the earliest schools was to instruct young persons in reading the Bible. After the Federal Land Act of 1785, a patchwork of townships was set in motion in the Northwest Territory with Section 16 reserved to financially support public education.

The Northwest Ordinance of 1787 further stated that "Religion, morality, and knowledge being necessary to good government and the happiness of mankind, schools and the means of education shall forever be encouraged." These same ideas and words were included in the first Ohio Constitution in 1802. Ohio's Constitution also stated that children would have access to public school regardless of their family's level of income.

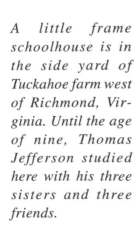

A little frame schoolhouse is in the side yard of Tuckahoe farm west of Richmond, Virginia. Until the age of nine, Thomas Jefferson studied here with his three sisters and three friends.

Even though Thomas Jefferson promoted public education, free public schools did not become a reality in Virginia until about 1870. For generations, landowners preferred to send their children to private academies. Pictured above is an early Shenandoah Valley school.

It was Thomas Jefferson who said that a free public education was a necessity for a democratic government. Jefferson had first introduced a bill in the Virginia Assembly in 1779 stating that education was essential to maintain liberty. This bill was the foundation of the state system of schools today.

> Certain forms of government are better calculated than others to protect individuals in the free exercise of natural rights, and are at the same time themselves better guarded against degeneracy, yet experience has shown that even under the best forms, those entrusted with power have, in time, and by slow operations, perverted it into tyranny; and it is believed that the most effectual means of preventing this would be, to illuminate, as far as practical, the minds of the people at large. . . .

Nowhere else was this democratic process practiced more closely than in the small, rural communities which surrounded the midwestern one-room schools. Farmers planned, constructed, supported, and cared for these buildings that educated their children. It was a simpler, less confusing time when America was a collection of tiny crossroads in the countryside. Yet, even today, one-room schools still symbolize the tradition of American education.

Buildings which have served a dedicated purpose for so long are hard to tear down. What the passing traveler today does not see is perhaps more significant. Beyond the physical evidence of the buildings and schoolyards left behind, the traveler must mentally picture the lessons learned, the friendships formed, and the memories shared by thousands of schoolchildren. Their world was once only as far as they could walk. It is their faces and their hopes and dreams which are mirrored by the side of the road.

Some One-Room Schools Survive Change

According to Andrew Gulliford in *America's Country Schools*, at the beginning of the twentieth century, there were still over 200,000 one-room country schools in the United States (233). Nearly half of them were located in the Midwest. By the end of World War II, the number had dwindled to 107,000 nationwide and 60,000 in the twelve midwestern states (Fuller 117). Because of the increasing urban population, advances in communication, and better modes of transportation, most country schools had ceased operating by the 1950s.

However, in the decade approaching the year 2000, some states with remote regions and fewer persons still educate children in one-room schools. Tamara Henry writes in *USA Today* that there are more than 1,600 open each school year. The wide-open spaces of

1924 photograph of a school class at Ramsey School, District No. 7, Center Township, Williams County, Ohio, with teacher Mabel Rinkel.

A white frame Amish schoolhouse still educates children in southern Hillsdale County, Michigan. Neighboring Amish farmers care for the building and grounds on a rural roadside.

An old German schoolhouse now houses the woodshop of an Amish furniture craftsman. Located in LaGrange County, Indiana, its frame siding has been unpainted for some time.

Nebraska claim the most. Some other states with numerous publicly-run one-room schools are Montana, South Dakota, Wyoming, North Dakota, and Florida. Surprisingly, in 1984, California still had over forty. The figure of 1,600 includes 708 Old Order Amish and Mennonite one-room schools and an additional 481 private schools.

There are hundreds more one-room school buildings that have been preserved as living history landmarks. These can be found in large

Walnut Run School in Lancaster County, Pennsylvania, dates back to 1878. Today, it is the only publicly-operated one-room school in that county even though the student body is mostly Amish.

numbers in the states previously mentioned and particularly in Colorado, Iowa, and Minnesota.

If something took place in the past, it can become more idealized and glorified as time goes by. We frequently hear the phrase, "Let's get back to the basics in education." While the widespread era of one-room schoolhouses is gone, there may be good things about them which should be remembered and reconsidered.

The Cahill School in Edina, Minnesota, built in 1864, was part of an early pioneer crossroads which also included a church. The Greek Revival building now serves as a living history museum for visiting school groups.

What positive elements of the one-room school classroom are still being used? And what former practices are currently missing from the experiences of today's children? The small classroom with multi-aged students progressing at their own rate and assisting each other may not be a new concept after all. A few things missing today in the lives of children are the family gatherings and conversations, the expected responsibilities and chores contributed by family members, the creative forms of entertainment in a culture without television or computers, and the existence of close-knit families and small neighborhoods where community events revolved around the school.

Surveyors Divide the Land

The Federal Land Act of 1785, inspired by Thomas Jefferson, first ordered a master plan for surveying the wilderness area beyond the Appalachian Mountains. The Northwest Territory would later become the states of Ohio, Indiana, Michigan, Illinois, Wisconsin, and the eastern part of Minnesota. The surveyors would shape the face of this land into an organized pattern of square units.

Ohio was the first area of land to be measured. After dividing the territory into north and south range lines, the surveyors measured townships of six miles squared. Each township was further divided into thirty-six smaller sections of 640 acres, which was one square mile. These square miles were then numbered from one to thirty-six, usually beginning from east to west. Alternate rows were numbered in the opposite direction.

By 1787, members of Congress had officially named these lands the Northwest Territory, and they had outlined a plan to govern the region. The numbered sections made it possible for the government to offer exact plots of land for sale. At first, settlers were required to buy an entire square mile at the price of one dollar an acre. Later, smaller pieces of land were available (Stewart 99-100). As new states formed in the Northwest Territory, every road, farm, church, and school location could be pinpointed on a map grid.

Section 16 of every township was set aside to help finance public schools. In Ohio, the legislature authorized the sale or rental of Section 16 at an auction. This designated land area totaled 700,000 acres (Wagner 32). The money collected was then paid to the State Treasury which gave six percent annually on the amount. These funds were available to each township to help build schools and pay teachers. Even though there were future problems, this funding plan provided a beginning for free public education.

Northwest Ohio Forms the Frontier

When the population of Ohio reached nearly 60,000 in the year 1803, Ohio was granted statehood. Ohio thus became the first state developed from the Northwest Territory. Because of many immigrants from Germany, the State Constitution was initially printed in both German and English. The earliest

A covered wagon pulled by oxen, such as this one, carried early pioneers across the Appalachian Mountains and into the Northwest Territory. Bows of hickory wood supported the canvas. The long, narrow wagon carried barrels and trunks of supplies on overland trails such as the National Road. It was often more comfortable for the travelers to walk beside the wagon.

pioneers journeyed west in flatboats on the Ohio River and in wagons on the National Road as they moved farther inland. Farms and villages gradually spread across the state, and the northwest corner of Ohio was the last area to be settled. A vast number of these settlers were German farmers (Good 181).

As the first white settlers arrived in Northwest Ohio, many Indians also claimed rights to the waterlogged wilderness. The heavily-wooded swampland, known as the Great Black Swamp, had delayed easy travel into the old Indian Territory. Soldiers first cut a road through at the outbreak of the War of 1812. In 1833, any Indians remaining were forced to move to Missouri because of a government order (Cooley and Maynard 9).

Williams County, Ohio's northwest corner, was first surveyed in 1820 and officially organized in 1824. This survey took place shortly before the Ohio-Michigan border dispute when boundaries between the two states

were questioned. Without bloodshed, in 1835 the border was finally moved north in favor of Ohio, increasing the land acreage in Williams County alone by 150 square miles (Rosevink 5).

Williams County was named for David Williams. Williams, along with two other men, had captured Major John Andre, a British spy during the War of 1812. At that time, according to an informational map from the engineers' office, Williams County was much larger in size. It encompassed land area to the south, which is now Defiance and Paulding Counties, and land area to the east, which is now part of Fulton, Putnam, and Henry Counties. Putnam and Henry Counties separated from Williams County in 1834, and Paulding County formed in 1839. In 1845, Defiance County was begun, and by 1850, Fulton County was organized. Thus, Williams County was finally reduced to its present twelve townships of 421 square miles.

A log school replica has been recreated at the site of Ohio's first settlement in 1772 at Schoenbrunn Village in northeastern Ohio.

The few schools in Ohio before 1820 were private ones. Only parents who could afford the extra expense of one to three dollars per term sent their children to school. The law to establish schools and provide children with a free public education in Ohio was passed in 1825. Ohio's 1840 census lists 407,466 children between the ages of six and fifteen. Only forty percent attended any kind of school (Norton 47).

Each school district covered six or seven sections in a township. After the state incorporated such an area as

In contrast, a modern stone high school educates students today outside Stow, Ohio.

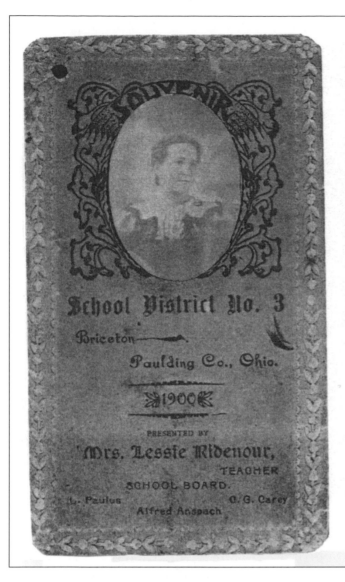

SOUVENIR

School District No. 3

Briceton

Paulding Co., Ohio.

1900

PRESENTED BY

Mrs. Lessie Ridenour,
TEACHER

SCHOOL BOARD.

L. Paulus   O. G. Carey
Alfred Anspach

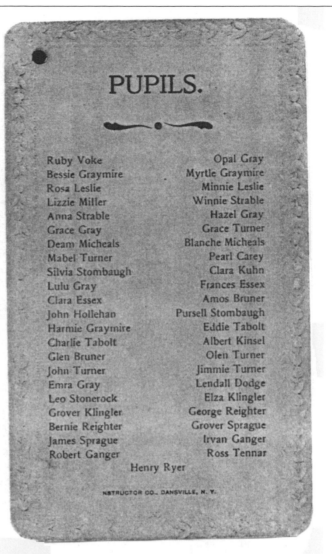

PUPILS.

Ruby Voke	Opal Gray
Bessie Graymire	Myrtle Graymire
Rosa Leslie	Minnie Leslie
Lizzie Miller	Winnie Strable
Anna Strable	Hazel Gray
Grace Gray	Grace Turner
Deam Micheals	Blanche Micheals
Mabel Turner	Pearl Carey
Silvia Stombaugh	Clara Kuhn
Lulu Gray	Frances Essex
Clara Essex	Amos Bruner
John Hollehan	Pursell Stombaugh
Harmie Graymire	Eddie Tabolt
Charlie Tabolt	Albert Kinsel
Glen Bruner	Olen Turner
John Turner	Jimmie Turner
Emra Gray	Lendall Dodge
Leo Stonerock	Elza Klingler
Grover Klingler	George Reighter
Bernie Reighter	Grover Sprague
James Sprague	Irvan Ganger
Robert Ganger	Ross Tennar

Henry Ryer

INSTRUCTOR CO., DANSVILLE, N. Y.

Students at the First Briceton School.

School House,
Briceton, Ohio.

Briceton School—a two-story frame building—was District No. 3 in Blue Creek Township, Paulding County, Ohio. It was replaced by a one-story brick school in 1910.

a school district, the farmers and families who lived there took over as shareholders. This arrangement helped the rural citizens give order to their lives. The schoolhouse became the center of the community, and decisions about how to run it and how to maintain it belonged to those who lived within the district's boundaries.

*Bow gracefully and respectfully
on entering and leaving the schoolroom
and before any recitation when a teacher is present.*

Chapter 2

Log Schools

Early Settlers Provide 3 Rs

*The notched ends of logs fit together to
form the walls of a log schoolhouse. Mud
and clay filled the cracks between logs and
also held the stone chimney in place.*

Pioneer schools were crude log
structures built soon after a forest area
was cleared. The school was usually one
of the first public buildings constructed
in a village. Many times it also served
as a church or a meeting place. Schools
were sometimes built on land unfit for
any other use.

Settlers in a school district met
together to plan the work of building
these one-room log schools. They worked
cooperatively to cut down trees, haul
wood, and hew logs to shape the beams
and rafters. Frontiersmen notched the
ends of logs to stack for the outer walls,
and they filled in cracks with mud and
clay or split sticks and straw. Windows
were crudely cut and then covered with
greased paper. Builders hung the thick
plank door on wooden hinges. The floors
were either dirt or puncheon, which was
the smoothed side of a log facing up.

Most log schools were heated by a
stone and mud fireplace at one end of the
room. Homemade writing tables made of
planks surrounded the inside edges of
the rough walls, facing the windows.
They were fastened in the wall at an
angle on wooden pins. Settlers sawed
logs in half and smoothed them on one
side to make seats. They mounted these
backless benches on flared wooden poles
high enough to reach the tables (Shinn
207).

Except for the basic hand-hewn
tables and benches, the pioneers
provided no other furnishings. The log
schools were not built for comfort. There
were no blackboards, framed pictures,
or fancy lamps on the walls (Fuller 9).

The teacher's desk inside this log school is like a wooden pulpit. Representing the 1836 era, the school is located in Prairietown at Conner Prairie Museum in Fishers, Indiana.

Wood writing tables were attached to the inside walls, and log benches faced the light provided by the long, narrow windows.

School was in session six days a week as pioneer students sat on these crude log benches. Children attended in winter when they weren't needed for chores at home. Since desks were absent, students recited their lessons aloud.

A student in a log school room sat facing the window while writing with slate on a frame board or while using a quill pen on homemade paper.

in homemade copy books using goose feather quill pens dipped in inkwells.

What about the teachers in these log schoolhouses? Known as schoolmasters or school-marms, they played many roles. Some were hired for their muscle rather than their scholastic ability. In addition to preparing daily lessons, they performed menial tasks such as stoking the fire each day with a fire poker and filling the kerosene lamps.

Most schoolmasters were not much older than their pupils, and they were usually not married.

The fireplace, with its uneven heat, made the air smoky and the walls discolored. Wind whistled through cracks as the students worked.

School materials were mostly homemade, and there were few books, possibly a Bible, a dictionary, and a hymnal. Students used hornbooks, or wooden paddles on which letters, numbers, and Bible verses were in-scribed. They practiced sums with charcoal on birchbark, or they used slate pencils on small slate boards. Students also wrote their lessons

The early schoolmaster, especially during the winter, was often a young male teacher who required strict discipline from his students.

A pail of water was carried in from an outside stream. Students shared a common dipper and tin drinking cup.

schedules, and they could not spend much time with each student. The teacher taught the younger students first, and ended with the older ones. Children worked at their desks, drilling and copying while they helped each other. Many classes were devoted to memorizing facts and reciting them in a sing-song fashion. Since there were so few books, students learned long Bible verses and poems. Lessons about moral behavior were common.

Students were expected to follow strict rules. The teacher swiftly punished misbehaving students by having them stand in a corner, wear a dunce cap, or balance themselves on blocks of wood. The teacher boxed their ears or whipped them with a leather strap or a birch switch (Kalman 25).

Besides receiving very little pay, they lived with the families of their students, often moving every few weeks. Their personal activities were closely monitored by members of the community. Sometimes the male minister also served as the teacher. Some men used teaching as a stepping-stone to another profession. After marriage, young female teachers were required to quit their jobs.

In a log schoolhouse, the school day was long. Teachers followed rigid

Candles provided one source of early lighting. If the fireplace died down, hand-held bellows could restore the flames.

The Raspberry School, built in 1896 by Norwegians in Bayfield County, Wisconsin, was used until 1914 at Raspberry Bay on Lake Superior. This log school was moved to Old World Wisconsin near Eagle in 1975. The State Historical Society restored the interior to the 1906 era.

Such methods of discipline were both embarrassing and painful.

Some schools were open only a few months a year. Children as young as three or four years of age attended with students up to twenty-one years old. Younger children went to school in the summer, and they were often taught by young women without much education themselves. Older children, especially boys, attended during the winter months when they had fewer farm chores to do. Usually a male teacher handled the older students. Thus, the early school calendar was divided into summer and winter terms (Good 206-207).

In the sparsely-settled woodlands, the frontiersmen truly wanted their children to learn. The pioneers had designed the log schoolhouses much like their log homes by using the same readily available trees. They had donated their back-breaking labor and dutifully provided a place for their children to study the three Rs of Reading, 'Riting, and Religion.

Villagers Construct First Schools

The first log schoolhouse in the most northwestern county of Ohio was built about 1837 in a village called

Denmark. This occurred only ten years after the first white settler came to Williams County when the total population was barely 400. Denmark was located a few miles northeast of the present town of Edgerton on an old Indian trail. Surveyed in 1834, Denmark was platted beside the St. Joseph River on land owned by a British storekeeper named Payne C. Parker. The village grew to include a tavern, a church, and the county's first post office (Cooley and Maynard 131-133).

Streets in Denmark were laid out and Judge Parker, who was a justice of the peace and a county commissioner, donated land for a public square. The log schoolhouse was built on the north side of the square under a large apple tree.

The Rev. Elijah Stoddard taught the first classes at the Denmark School in 1837-38. No doubt, reading Bible passages was a main part of the curriculum. Other subjects were reading from *McGuffey's Readers*, spelling, penmanship, and arithmetic. Classes lasted six hours a day. Parents furnished wood for the fireplace based on how many of their children were enrolled (Shinn 153-154).

One early resident of St. Joseph Township described his log school as "primitive with a clapboard roof held in place by ridge poles." He also said that each side of the school had a ten- or twelve-foot-long window. Seats and desks extended around the inside walls, and the writing desks were pinned to the wall with wooden pegs. Basswood log slabs, with the bark side turned down, formed the seats. The height of the legs made it difficult for smaller children to touch the floor. Students helped chop wood for the open fireplace at the far end (Goodspeed and Blanchard 360).

Soon other log schoolhouses were built in St. Joseph Township. It was as if the seeds of the first school had scattered in the wind and taken root.

Not all early settlements in Williams County thrived, and the plans of Judge Parker for the village of Denmark died when he did. Within thirty years, the village plat was vacated, and every trace of the village but the tavern disappeared. Today, a historical stone by an old chestnut tree marks the former site of the tavern. Thus, the entire village of Denmark and the first schoolhouse can only be found in record books (Cooley and Maynard 134).

Townships Organize School Districts

Not long after the school in Denmark was built, other townships in Williams County constructed their first log schools. These schools provided the nucleus for small crossroad villages. Many of these villages, like Denmark, are now gone, or they leave only a house or two where once a close-knit community flourished. In his 1905 book, *History of Williams County, Ohio*, William Shinn provides insight into these early schools (155-160).

In 1837, even before a town had been platted, the first school in Center Township was built. The school was a log cabin with a huge fireplace and a tall outside chimney. It also contained desks of rough boards placed on pins in the wall. The clapboard seats had legs made of wooden poles.

A two-story log house still stands in Williams County, Ohio—built ca1845 by early Ohio settler Jacob Young. In the 1970s, it was restored as a museum by the Williams County Historical Society.

A unique teacher in this school near Melbern was known as Old Man Barney. Barney received his pay by subscription, which meant that most of his wages came from tuition paid by the parents of students. Barney was described as "an odd fellow with peculiar habits" and yet as "a good teacher." His nickname was "Yankee," and he later taught at other log schools. One noted punishment at the Melbern School was tying students together and making them stand on their desks for long periods of time.

The early 1840s brought the beginning of school districts in eight other townships of Williams County. After the log schoolhouses were erected, the school district committees hired young teachers. When roads were developed and more areas of the county were settled, additional districts were established. As villages grew, the farmers would soon replace the first crude log buildings with more substantial frame or brick one-room schoolhouses.

In the winter of 1841, a small log schoolhouse was built near Billingstown in Northwest Township. A local resident, William H. Billings, was one of the builders. The first teacher on record was Miss Abigail Hills, who taught ten students for two or three months in 1841-42. During the school term, she married T.F. Whaley which thus ended her teaching career. Later, a brick school was built a half mile south of Billingstown. All that remains of the town today is a cemetery and a few houses.

Miss Mary McCrillus, described as "handsome, lively, and quite a flirt," was employed to teach a summer term at Bridgewater Township's first schoolhouse in 1841. The school was a rough log structure at the edge of a farm. On damp summer nights, Miss McCrillus often sat by the schoolhouse fire with her beau. Unfortunately, the next day she could not stay awake in front of her class. She fell asleep in her chair or stretched herself out on a seat only to be awakened by the mischief of her students. Due to these circumstances, she was dismissed from her teaching job.

In Jefferson Township, George Durbin taught in a log schoolhouse near the corner where Hillside Country Living is now located. The logs of the school were described as small, and the door was made of clapboard.

By 1841, Jefferson Township was divided into twelve school districts. The amount paid to teachers ranged from $12 to $20 per month, and the teachers boarded with the parents of their students. Reports reveal that corporal punishment was practiced in all districts. Standard materials in use were the *Elementary Spelling Book*, *Emerson's Readers*, *Olney's Geography*, and *Kirkham's Grammar Books*. Spelling schools were a popular activity,

Lockport School District No. 7, Brady Township, Williams County, Ohio.

and students often competed with neighboring school districts to see who had the best spellers (Goodspeed and Blanchard 475).

According to Abraham Gish in Brady Township, a "20- by 26-foot-long house with a window on each side, an open fireplace, and a pioneer stick chimney outside" first housed several terms of the Lockport School. In 1845, a solid frame schoolhouse set on oak blocks was built for $160. Mrs. Mary Shipman taught the first session there with two terms held each year.

Several other schoolhouses in Lockport were built on the same site as the frame school. This was done either to improve the school or to replace a building after it had been ravaged by fire (Cooley and Maynard 62). This cycle of rebuilding schools was common as small villages sought ways to better the condition of the buildings which educated their children.

Two of the last townships in Williams County to organize school districts were Millcreek and Springfield Townships. Settlements there were close together, and school districts were not started in some areas until the need for them. Miss Sarah Jones said she taught in Springfield Township in the winter of 1850-51 for $2 per week, which was considered a big price. Gentlemen received as much as $3 to $4 per week. Both men and women teachers boarded around with the families of scholars (Goodspeed and Blanchard 439).

Some towns, such as Alvordton, sprang up when the Wabash Railroad passed through. Other towns, such as Primrose, eventually died off because the village was not part of the railroad's path.

Chapter 3

Oh! we may get weary,
And think work is dreary;
'Tis harder by far
To have nothing to do.
Marian Douglas

School Laws

Rules Organize Districts

Ohio was the first state to use land endowment to support public education. The 1825 public school law gave school districts the authority to elect a district school committee and appoint a school examiner. School districts could also levy a one-half mill tax on each dollar of land evaluation. But, most landowners either objected to the school tax or preferred to keep their children home to work. Parents felt that both boys and girls could learn needed life skills at home.

In 1853, the state set a two-mill levy for schools. This opened free schools to every child. Later, a ten-mill limitation was enacted. Any further taxes required a vote by the taxpayers.

In 1837, when the first log school in Williams County was under construction, the State Legislature appointed the first State Superintendent of Schools. Like a circuit-riding preacher, he spent a year riding the rural roads of Ohio on horseback. He traveled from village to village to spread the message of free public schools. During the day, the Honorable Samuel Lewis visited schoolhouses, and in the evening, he spoke to community groups. Besides slavery, the issue of free schools was the most hotly debated topic in the early 1800s (Norton 51).

Due to the influence of Samuel Lewis, an 1838 state law organized a system of county school superintendents and township inspectors. Their role was to enforce school laws and report back to the State Superintendent (Thomas 14-15). Also, in 1838, a State Common School Fund for adequate school funding was enacted (Sheeley 3).

Around 1850, school districts were set up within a boundary of four square miles. This meant that a school was located near the district's center, or every two miles in the county. Thus, few students had to go more than a mile to school. Certain county roads and corners were designated on county plat maps as locations for school buildings.

Citizens in a school district elected a school board made up of three directors. Nearly every farmer had an opportunity to serve on the school board. The board presided at school meetings and hired teachers. Boards

This brick one-room school south of Pittsburgh, Pennsylvania, now serves patrons as the Classroom Restaurant. Menus are written on slate boards.

also reported enrollments to the county superintendent, purchased school supplies, authorized school repairs, and paid the bills (Fuller 4-5). Members of the board had a say in determining curriculum and textbooks. The process was a small-scale democracy in action.

For example, the first school district east of the village of West Unity was known as the Combs School (Thomas 78). The following information is from the Combs School secretary's book:

In February 1848, Benjamin Combs and his family arrived here from Richland County, Ohio. In April, he went to Moses Bates' house to discuss with the voters of the district to get a schoolhouse built. Householders were to elect three school directors, a secretary and treasurer. They were allowed to impose their own tax for the erection of the building.

April 8, 1848, Benjamin Combs was chosen to be chairman of the school board. Resolutions were as follows:

1) Resolved that sum of $200 be assessed to build a schoolhouse.

2) Resolved that one-half of the tax to be paid on the 16th of October next, 1848.

Built in 1858, the Little Red Schoolhouse in Poland Township, Ohio, first served as a subscription school. Students paid a fee of money or goods in order to attend. The school can now be rented for special events.

3) Resolved that the other half be paid one year from the first of October 1848.

4) Resolved that the building be painted white.

5) Resolved that the building be in size 20 feet by 26 feet.

Lumber was hauled from a water-powered mill in Montpelier. The sealing was hauled from the Lockport Mill. All the voters helped erect the building during the winter. A fence was built around the lot, and a little outhouse was erected on both back corners.

The first frame schoolhouses were rectangular in shape with a steep, gabled roof, white clapboard siding, and three uniform windows on each of the longer sides. Hay Jay School, last used as a school in 1957, is preserved and owned by the Williams County (Ohio) Historical Society.

Chapter 4

At the crossroads of section sixteen it stood
On a prominent rise of ground.
'Twas a sturdy white frame structure
And could be viewed from miles around.

Roscoe E. Armstrong

School Structures
Frame and Brick Replace Logs

The wooden frame schoolhouses which followed the log ones were uniform buildings designed by the farmers who built them. Typically, the schools were about thirty by fifty feet in size with horizontal clapboard siding, cedar shingles, and a gabled roof at each end (Gulliford 172). In the Midwest, wood was the most common building material.

Building a frame schoolhouse was like building the studs and joists on a barn. Few formal blueprints were necessary because farmers merely agreed on its foundation and size. Usually built in just a few weeks, the school was a rectangular-shaped framework of studs and sills with three windows on each side and a door at the front. A brick fireplace and chimney or an iron stove was placed at the back.

Most frame schools were white because white paint was cheaper than red. The typical schoolhouse had no shutters or fancy trim. There was little or no insulation between the walls. The creaky wood floors were solid pine. Even though such frame schools were similar, there were always small differences which gave each school its own identity. Improvements such as cloak rooms, porches, and bell towers occurred in the late 1800s.

In addition to building the schoolhouse, farmers also bore the work and cost of providing outhouses, or restrooms. In the days of log schools, groves of trees probably served as private places. Some schools had only one outhouse which had to be shared alternately by girls and then boys at recess breaks. But, most schools had two outhouses, one for boys and one for girls. Some outhouses were built of brick to match the school, but most were just small frame structures with steeply sloping roofs. High board fences sometimes shielded the entrances.

Many outhouses could accommodate only one person at a time, but there were also two- and three-seaters. In some instances, there was a low seat for the primary-aged children, and two higher seats for the bigger children. In the gabled ends of the roof, openings were cut to allow fresh air and light. Also, a supply of catalogs, kept in a flat

Outhouses were sometimes constructed from the same building material as the schoolhouses. The sloping roofs on the outhouses allowed for ventilation. Most outhouses were located on back corners of the school lots. Walnut Run School (above) is near Strasburg, Lancaster County, Pennsylvania.

This white frame school and matching outhouse are located at Auglaize Village near Defiance, Ohio.

wooden box, served as toilet paper (Thomas 84).

Plans for sanitary outhouses were not widely promoted by state officials until the early 1900s. Previous outhouses were unclean and in disrepair. Through the years, some had been badly neglected or vandalized (Gulliford 175).

In a book called *The Rural School Plant*, the following advice was distributed by the State Superintendent of Schools:

> There should always be separate toilets for the sexes, and they should be far enough apart to avoid moral contagion. The main considerations are privacy and cleanliness. A latticed enclosure in front of the door . . . is always desirable.

At one point before 1855, the advantages of the round or octagonal school building were promoted. Such a design was thought to be compact and efficient. With an iron stove placed in the center of the octagon, the room could be more evenly heated. Each side of the octagon featured either a window or a doorway. Student desks could be placed around the outside walls, some facing the wall and some facing the center of the room. Over seventy pupils could be accommodated. The teacher's desk usually sat in front of the doorway, facing the students. Students could easily be separated by grade levels.

The fad of building octagon-shaped schools was most popular in the East. Octagon school buildings were built in the states of New Jersey, New York, Delaware, and particularly Pennsylvania (Gulliford 173). None were ever constructed in Northwest Ohio, but a few scattered ones could be found in other states.

This brick octagonal school was built in 1873 in Sparta, Illinois. Called Charter Oak School, it was used as a public school until 1953. The unique structure has been restored and furnished as a school museum.

The Eight Square Schoolhouse in Bedford County, Pennsylvania, has been relocated to Old Bedford Village. Built in 1851, the frame school served a Quaker community.

Such an idea did not have much success with midwestern farmers. Even when brick became the common building material in the 1880s, the basic one-room rectangular shape of schools did not change. By then, however, there were various suggested building plans available from the state.

Some later schools, with their anterooms, bell towers, and separate front entrances, closely resembled churches. Most schools were built in a short period of time, and their size was still determined by the range of one teacher's voice.

In the late 1800s, red-brick schoolhouses were made from clay brick. Sometimes, the brick was baked

The inside of the octagon schoolhouse provided more wall space for desks. Recitation benches were placed in front of each grade level.

These two schoolhouses with their tall bell towers closely resemble church buildings. The entrance to Collins School (above), built in 1877 in Steuben County, Indiana, is on the left side while the false door on the right side adds symmetry. The restored school is owned by a former pupil and teacher at the school—June Collins.

Sherry School in Defiance County, Ohio, was built in a classic style in the mid-1800s. The frame structure was moved a mile north to become part of a historical village.

Jackson Township Hall, in the restored Canal town of Roscoe Village in Ohio, was built in 1880. Used as a school in 1911, it was restored as a school museum in 1971.

in kilns right on site. Brick provided sturdy school buildings. Red-brick schools also promoted the term "Little Red Schoolhouse."

Besides brick from local kilns for the walls, farmers used hardwood wainscoting halfway up the inside walls, and then they plastered the upper half of the inside walls. The symmetrical brick structures, with their standard gabled roofs, faced the roadways. The school usually had an overhanging shelter above the front door.

Brick schools were permanently located on their foundations. But, frame buildings could easily be placed on skids and moved to neighboring districts. This was often done to replace a build-

The first Boyd School in Holmes County, Ohio, was a frame structure in use from 1863 to 1889. Listed in the National Register of Historic Places, the brick Boyd School educated students from 1889-1952. Its name was derived from the Boyd family who still own the land and the school.

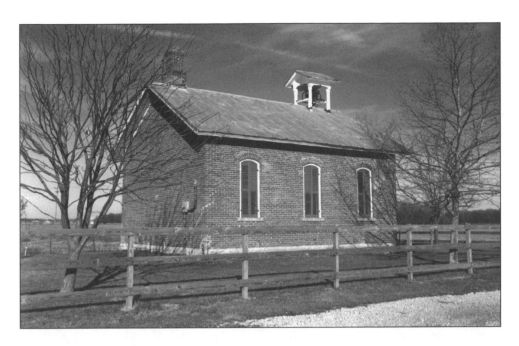

The Little Red School-house east of Findlay, Ohio, in Marion Township, was used from about 1860 to 1936. After a second life as a grain storage building, the school was donated to the Hancock County Historical Society and refurnished to its original state by 1973.

ing which had burned or to house a shift in school population.

Unlike early log schools, desks were now placed in rows in the middle of the room. Windows, which opened from the top, let in more light and air. Large iron stoves with pipes provided ventilation and replaced the stone fireplaces. Wall pictures and educational tools first made an appearance.

Textbooks, which followed a graded course of study, greatly enhanced student learning. There were readers, spellers, and grammar books. Several of the texts were written by college professors from Ohio. These men were William H. McGuffey (*McGuffey's Eclectic Readers*), Dr. Joseph Ray (*Ray's Arithmetic*), and Thomas W. Harvey (*Harvey's Grammar*).

This abandoned red brick schoolhouse in Ohio stands alone at a country cross-road in southern Paulding County. It has an inset arched entry.

This brick school was formerly District No. 6 located near Norwalk, Ohio. It now stands in Bowling Green, Ohio, on the campus of Bowling Green State University. First built in 1875, it was remodeled several times over the years. In 1974, the school was dismantled brick by brick, including the foundation and the eighteen-foot cupola. Through the efforts of an education professor, the schoolhouse now serves as an Educational Memorabilia Center.

Chapter 5

"What makes the lamb love Mary so?"
The eager children cried.
"Oh, Mary loved the lamb, you know,"
The teacher quick replied.

Sarah Hale

School Names
Labels Originate Many Ways

The names of one-room country schools, especially in Williams County, are an interesting study in themselves. Floyd Gardner, a former one-room school teacher, researched school names and sites for the Williams County Historical Society. Many schools were named for the villages where they were located such as Columbia or Hamer. Some names merely reflected the color or shape of the building such as Round School and Brick School. The most common origin of country school names was the name of the land donor. A close second was probably the name of the family with the most children in attendance.

Some schoolhouses were named after small villages in Williams County (Cooley 4). A few examples are Bridgewater Center, Columbia, Lockport, and Melbern. Additional ones are Primrose, Pulaski, Union Corners, West Jefferson, and Williams Center. Some of these villages are now completely gone, or they have only a few houses, a church, and a building with an abandoned storefront.

Often, schools were named for the farmer providing the ground for the building. Some names derived in this way in Williams County were Beatty, Cogswell, Doty, and Favourite. Other land doners included Malcolm, Ramsey, Schlegel, Schmachtenberger, Snow, Weber, and Witt.

Several other methods of naming a school were also utilized. A few schools were named in conjunction with a nearby church or grange hall such as Valley View (church) and Sodom (grange hall). Other school names depicted a nearby stream or lake such as Fish Creek, Yellow Run, and Nettle Lake. Or, school names described natural land forms including Clay Bank, Stony Point, and School Noll. A few names related to trees like Hickory Grove and Maple Grove. Certain country schools had two names or name changes through the years such as Leatherwood/Julliard and Greenwood/McConeghy.

The most frequently used school name by school boards in the Midwest was Pleasant (Gulliford 35). Williams

Pleasant Valley School District No. 7 in Walnut Creek Township, Holmes County, Ohio, in 1917.

County alone had five such schools. Superior Township had two schools named Pleasant Hill. Hay Jay School in Bridgewater Township was also known as Pleasant Hill. In addition, there was a Pleasant Grove in Jefferson Township and a Pleasant Grove in Northwest Township.

Other school names in Williams County were also duplicated. Both Center Township and Florence Township had a Jerusalem School. And, both Jefferson Township and Madison Township had a Center School. Millcreek had Clay School; Jefferson had Clay Bank School; and Superior had Clay Corners School.

Some of the more unusual names for one-room schools in Williams County were Yackee, Prospect, Stringtown, Basswood Deerlick, and Devil's Half Acre. Names of schools, of course,

reflected the pride of citizens in their district. District numbers were usually posted on the school above the entrance or inscribed on a cornerstone, along with the year the school was constructed.

Two one-room schools in Williams County currently serve as museums and are furnished to represent their original state. One of these is Center School, a red-brick building on County Roads J and 16 in Jefferson Township, last used in 1956. Center School is overseen by the county commissioners and is part of Opdycke Park. The other museum is Hay Jay School, located on County Road 8 between County Roads R and S in Bridgewater Township. Hay Jay, a white frame building, is part of the Williams County Historical Society. Hay Jay was last used as a public school in 1957. The schools are open by appointment to visitors and school groups.

Chapter 6

Blessings on thee, little man,
Barefoot boy, with cheeks of tan!
With thy turned-up pantaloons,
And thy merry whistled tunes.

John Greenleaf Whittier

The Walk To School

Students Create Adventures

Former one-room school students fondly remember the walk to and from school. Since there were no school buses with scheduled routes, the walk itself posed an exciting adventure in all kinds of weather. The path from home to school may have led down a farm lane, across a cow pasture, over clear-running creeks, or through fields of ripening crops. Such shortcuts provided close-up glimpses of science lessons.

Children walked along country roads in groups of two or three as they carried their lunch pails and perhaps a book. Because children lived far apart on farms, they welcomed the chance to leave chores behind and join their friends. The company of playmates made the mile or two journey seem much shorter.

The walk to school varied with each season of the year. In spring, rain muddied the roads and made them difficult to navigate. Boys in bibbed overalls and girls in cotton dresses got quite wet wading across overflowing creeks. In summer, wildflowers, butterflies, and small animals captured their attention and caused various detours.

In the fall, children stopped by the roadside to pick sprigs of bittersweet for their teacher. Or, they jumped in piles of leaves.

Children walked in twos and threes along the roadside enroute to and from school. Built in 1883, this school was District No. 5 in German Township, Fulton County, Ohio.

Amish children enjoy sledding in the snows of winter. Horses which they have ridden to school feed in the brisk outdoors.

Gunnary School near Annadale, Minnesota, stands serenely beside one of Minnesota's many lakes. The white frame building, now a home, has a steep roof and gazebo-shaped bell tower.

An early 1900s Defiance County, Ohio, schoolteacher, Rosa Valet, hitched up her horse each morning for the ride to school.

Schools never closed in the snowstorms of winter. Students clothed themselves in layers of long underwear, leggings, coats, stocking caps, and mittens. They may have been transported by sleigh over banks of snow or in wagons pulled by horses. The warm clothing prevented frostbite. Some brave souls rode bicycles on ice.

A few lucky students rode ponies to school. Some children made the daily trip by hitching horses to carts. During the day, the horses required care and feeding (Webb 99). This activity provided another source of entertainment for students at recess.

Walking to and from school was a creative adventure for country schoolchildren. Friendships flowered and pranks were instigated. The journey was a time of camaraderie and mischief at the beginning and end of the school day.

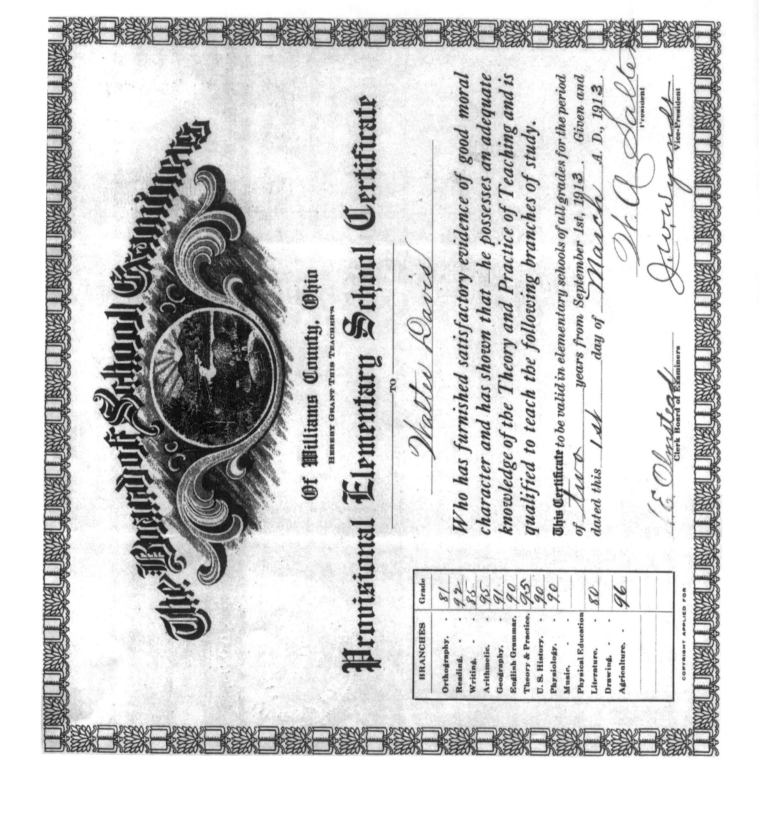

The Board of School Examiners

Of Williams County, Ohio

HEREBY GRANT THIS TEACHERS

Provisional Elementary School Certificate

TO

Walter Davis

Who has furnished satisfactory evidence of good moral character and has shown that __he possesses an adequate knowledge of the Theory and Practice of Teaching and is qualified to teach the following branches of study.

This Certificate to be valid in elementary schools of all grades for the period of _Two_ years from September 1st, 1913. Given and dated this _1st_ day of _March_ A. D., 1913.

H. A. Salen
President

_____
Vice-President

_____
Clerk Board of Examiners

BRANCHES	Grade
Orthography,	81
Reading,	72
Writing,	25
Arithmetic,	95
Geography,	91
English Grammar,	90
Theory & Practice,	95
U. S. History,	90
Physiology,	90
Music,	
Physical Education	
Literature,	80
Drawing,	
Agriculture,	96

COPYRIGHT APPLIED FOR

Chapter 7

*A little of you lives in every child
with whom you come in contact.*

One-Room Schools
The Teacher and the Classroom

Even in one-room schools, the success of the students depended not only on the teacher's abilities, but on the support and resources of the local community. Before 1880, the only experience and certification a teacher needed was to successfully pass the eighth-grade test. Many young women then began to teach in the very same one-room school which they had attended.

After 1880, the General Assembly enacted the first state laws requiring teacher certification. Minimum qualifications were to be at least sixteen years old and of good moral character. Later, a state-appointed board of examiners conducted written tests for potential teachers. The tests covered all subjects taught in country schools. Formal teacher training did not begin until the early 1900s.

After the teacher received a certificate, she was employed by the township board of directors. He or she met briefly with the local school board to discuss the duties and terms of the contract. Besides teaching duties, the school board outlined janitorial tasks. They also clarified rules about teacher apparel and conduct. A salary of perhaps a dollar a day was agreed upon by both parties. If the teacher could not perform all the jobs such as building a fire by seven o'clock a.m. and scrubbing the wood floor weekly, a janitor's fee was deducted from the salary (Thomas 73). The teacher was now ready to start an assignment in a one-room classroom with fifteen up to forty children.

To begin, the teacher may have gotten assistance from a book such as Welch's *Teachers' Classification Register*. First published in 1884, it was used as a teacher's guide book. It contained advice on how to arrange the daily schedule and divide the students into primary, intermediate, and upper grades. The book listed subjects to be taught at each grade level and gave suggestions for instruction. The guide also offered methods of record keeping, although a standard system of grading was not developed until about 1890. In the record book, the teacher listed names of students, their grade levels, and brief comments about the textbooks used with them (Fuller 65-67).

In the early days, teachers usually taught no more than a term at each school. According to retired teacher

RULES FOR TEACHERS

☞ **DUTIES**

(Before or After School Session)

★ Wash windows & clean classroom with soap and water once a week.

★ Check outhouses daily. *(Plenty of old catalogues are available at School Board office.)*

☞ **APPAREL**

(Forbidden Wear in Public at All Times)

★ WOMEN: (1) A bathing costume
(2) Bloomers for cycling
(3) Skirts slit to expose ankles
(4) Bustle extension over 10 inches

★ MEN: (1) Detachable collar & neck tie removed from shirt
(2) Shirt sleeves unlinked & rolled
(3) Hair closely cropped *(unless bald or have disease of the scalp)*

☞ **CONDUCT**

(Cause for Immediate Dismissal)

★ Smoking of cigarettes, use of spirits, frequenting of pool or public dance halls.

★ Marriage or other unseemly behavior by women teachers.

★ Joining of any Feminist Movement, such as the *Suffragettes*.

JC Wayne

Superintendent—Sept. 15, 1886

Margaret Meyer Schurtz, a German immigrant, started the first U.S. kindergarten in this white frame building in 1856. Moved to this site by the Historical Society in 1956, the school is located in Watertown, Wisconsin. One-room schools in America, however, typically offered only grades one through eight.

Grace Geesey, school directors would then rotate the teacher to another school and class. Perhaps this practice prevented the teachers and students from getting too familiar. Each departing teacher had to write a year-end report for the teacher who would follow.

The teacher exemplified many talents as she led her charges in daily lessons. Besides teacher, she played the role of disciplinarian, nurse, counselor, janitor, and school administrator.

Prior to 1847, classes were not organized by grade levels, but by general levels of ability. Students from the ages of six to sixteen had lessons tailored to meet their needs. The school calendar included a summer term from May to September and a winter term from

November to April. The schedule reflected times when young boys were

Children as young as three or four years old sometimes attended one-room schools. They came with older brothers and sisters in the spring and summer months.

One-room school teachers played many roles and prepared daily lessons in all basic subjects for grades one through eight.

not needed to plant or harvest crops on the farm.

The teacher had to plan individualized lessons, taking into account a student's age and the times when he would be in attendance. Beginners started in the primer as their main text. Children were not allowed to have readers until they could spell. Then, each child worked at his own pace to be promoted from reader to reader, with the Fifth Reader being the highest (Good 207). Students overheard the teacher presenting lessons to other groups. Reading was the main emphasis, and the teacher planned about

forty daily lessons to accommodate a class of twenty students (Thomas 86). To meet these demands, the teacher encouraged older students to assist the younger ones in a relaxed, family-like atmosphere.

In 1847, the Ohio State Legislature enacted the "Akron Laws." This educational plan set up a system of eight grade levels in the public schools. The new plan meant that the busy teacher in the one-room school now had to prepare separate lessons for all eight grades in the basic areas of reading, spelling, writing, and arithmetic. Often, the basics for older students also

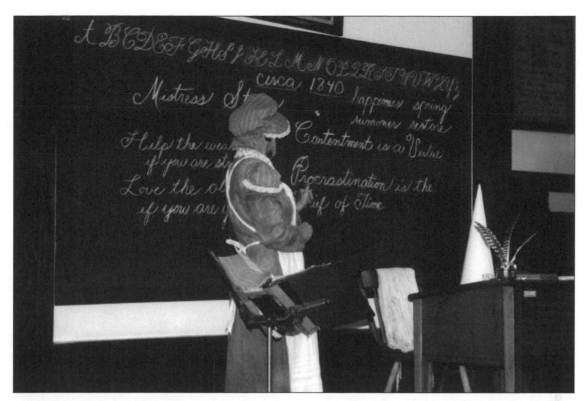

One-room school classes are re-enacted each year for all third graders in the Akron, Ohio, area schools. The Old Stone School, built in 1840, is the site of Akron, Ohio's, first public school. Before its 1967 restoration, it also served as a railroad office, Lutheran school, tool shed, and storehouse.

A log cabin depicts education on the Ohio frontier from 1825 to 1850. This cabin is located on the grounds of Hale Farm and Village located north of Akron, Ohio.

included grammar, geography, history, and hygiene.

When guidelines were met, the students were passed to the next higher grade. The teacher kept a record of the ability and progress of each child. It was common for students to skip grade levels or for some grade levels to be missing (Fuller 46-47). There were usually at least six grades represented in a classroom with two or three students in each grade (Webb 1).

After eighth grade, students took the county examination in order to graduate. For some, this marked the end of their formal education. For others, especially after 1900, an eighth-grade diploma signified entry into the nearest town's high school. Local county school boards were responsible for paying the tuition for their high school students. But, each parent had to arrange his own child's transportation into town.

Let The Lessons Begin!

During the typical school day in a one-room school, the teacher called children from the playground by ringing the nine o'clock bell. Students lined up outside the door to greet the teacher. Raising the U.S. flag on a pole in front of the school was an important ritual. Students then scrambled inside to hang their jackets on coat hooks against the wall and set their tin lunch pails on overhanging shelves.

In Rosevink's *History of Defiance County, Ohio*, school day activities are outlined (153-155). Opening exercises included the Pledge of Allegiance and the Lord's Prayer. If a pump organ or piano

The teacher called each grade level to come to the recitation bench in front of the room. Students had to recite aloud and answer questions. Students doing seat work at their desks could also hear the lessons of other grade levels.

was part of the furnishings, the class would sing a patriotic song below portraits of George Washington and Abraham Lincoln. Sometimes, in the Midwest, the opening also included a Bible reading and the singing of a hymn.

Because of the lessons to be covered, the teacher quickly began the daily routine. Work assignments were already written on the board for different grade levels. The teacher pointed them out and checked that each student had his proper materials.

The red brick Aztalan School, used until 1956, replaced an early yellow clay brick school and an even earlier frame structure which had burned. Built in 1918, the school has been restored and is part of the Aztalan Historical Museum near Lake Mills, Wisconsin.

Typical school furnishings of an early 1900s school are inside the Aztalan School. Note the iron stove, the pump organ, dark green window shades, and wood desks bolted to the floor. Aztec Indians who built pyramid-shaped mounds once lived near the school, and the site has been designated as a National Landmark.

As students did seat work, the teacher rang a brass handbell and called forward one grade level at a time. Each group sat on the long, wooden recitation bench in front of the blackboard as they recited lessons and answered questions. Students read aloud to the teacher, wrote on the board, and sounded out letters of words all in the space of ten minutes or before the next grade level came to the bench. For some subjects, the teacher combined grade levels. Rote learning, memorization, reading aloud, and copying were the methods of education.

The metal school bell signaled students for their lessons and also for their recess and lunch breaks.

Fortunately, by then, textbooks were designed to help students progress from one level to the next. In country schools, reading was the most important subject. William H. McGuffey, a Presbyterian minister, published six volumes of readers and spellers which were widely used in the Midwest, beginning in 1836 and into the twentieth century. The first McGuffey books contained literature by great English and American authors. Moral values and lessons were closely intertwined with stories and poems. Lessons stressed the virtues of honesty, hard work, courage, and persistence. The reading texts also included stories about history and patriotism.

While the teacher worked with one grade level in front, other sounds

Students from each grade level diligently took a turn at the recitation bench for each of their subjects. Here, students are reading from a graded reading series.

of activity filled the back of the room. The squeak of chalk on slates, the whisper of students working together, and the voices of younger children reading to older children were noticeable. Younger students had helpers assigned to them to answer their questions. Between her meetings with various groups, the teacher walked up and down the aisles to check the progress of seat work.

When the whole class finished their reading groups, it was time for a fifteen-minute morning recess and outhouse break. Students drank from

Students used a common dipper to get drinks from a water crock. Few were then aware that such a practice spread germs more readily.

a large water crock by using a shared tin dipper to fill their cups. After being confined in their seats, they were ready for the physical activity of group games.

Typical outdoor games such as Ante, Ante, Over the Shanty; Crack the Whip; Tag; and Red Rover involved students of all ages. Playing fair, taking turns, and being good sports were expected. Younger children played Ring Around the Rosy, London Bridge, and Blind Man's Bluff. Children stayed within earshot of the school so they

This porcelain water crock on a stand can be found inside the 1882 Stoen School at Gibbs Farm Museum, St. Paul, Minnesota. Another corner held a wash basin, pitcher, and mirror.

could hear the bell at the end of recess. The teacher did not always accompany the students outside.

Next on the day's agenda were the arithmetic lessons. For younger students, arithmetic was a subject to memorize, particularly the tables from two to twelve. Rules and poems helped students remember the facts. They practiced drills on hand-held slates. The teacher led math ciphering races at the board. Sometimes, the Sears and Roebuck catalog was used to create math problems. The teacher gave older students story problems about situations on the farm.

Ray's Arithmetic, a math program developed by Dr. Joseph Ray, was a popularly-used math series. The books began with simple numbers and advanced to harder problems about percentages, interest rates, and systems of weight. The first arithmetic texts were merely reference books, but later texts included graded levels of difficulty.

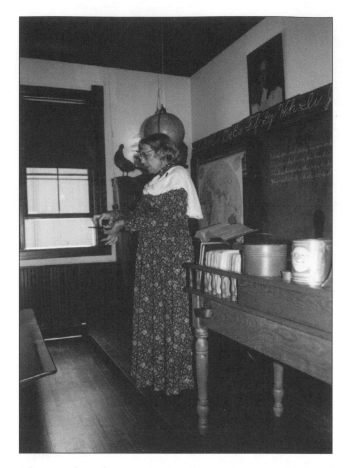

The teacher demonstrates the proper way to hold a pen while practicing penmanship skills. She stands on a raised platform in front of the class.

Cursive writing, or penmanship, required a great deal of time and effort. The teacher demonstrated the proper position for sitting and holding the pen. Shaping the letters and periodically dipping the tip of the pen in an inkwell was

Lunch was often stored in a tin pail or bucket above the coat rack. Many of these had previously served as containers for lard or syrup.

This early wooden swingset also included a swinging saddle.

tedious. Because of the fancy stroke patterns, some letters closely resembled others. Students practiced penmanship in writing pads as desk work.

In 1894, the Palmer method of ovals and slanted lines was introduced. This method of writing improved the speed, uniformity, and readability of students' handwriting. A set of letter cards above the blackboard provided an easy reference when writing sayings such as, "Small strokes fell mighty oaks."

At noon, classes stopped for the lunch-hour break. The teacher dismissed students by rows to get their tin lunch pails, which may have had previous lives as lard buckets or syrup pails. Or,

students carried their lunches in baskets or in paper wrapped with twine. To follow rules of good hygiene, everyone washed his hands in a basin filled with water. In winter, students sat at their desks to eat. But, in warm weather, children spread out in the school yard and swapped lunch items with their friends (Rosevink 154-157).

Lunches brought from home were not fancy. For a main course, lunch might have included slabs of meat such as cold bacon or sausage with bread and biscuits. Other frequently packed items were pieces of fruit, hard-boiled eggs, slices of cheese, and homemade cookies. One popular way to produce a hot lunch

An old-fashioned school yard surrounds this yellow brick Amish school in Holmes County, Ohio.

was to place a potato on the pot-bellied stove early in the day. By noon, the potato smelled quite appetizing and was ready to eat. Some children carried milk in a jar, but a thermos was unknown (Webb 50-53).

After lunch, students organized longer games such as rounder, a game similar to baseball. They used home-made bats and yarn balls with rubber cores (Good 216). Sometimes, the teacher participated in the games. There was time to play marbles and jacks. Since there was no playground equipment prior to the late 1800s, most recess games involved running and jumping, such as jump rope and hopscotch, or toys made at home. Children had to invent and adapt their own activities.

Back in the classroom, the afternoon began with a reading by the teacher. Then, the teacher called small groups for grammar, geography, and history classes. Grammar meant study-ing sentence structure and parts of speech. Students showed their under-standing by diagramming, or parsing, sentences on the board.

Studying state history was popu-lar, but other history was largely ignored. Even after 1870, history basi-cally covered events in North America. Lessons included geography, or locating the shapes of states and countries. However, available maps were not very accurate. Memorizing geographical facts fit in well with learning methods in a one-room school.

Another fifteen-minute recess occurred mid-afternoon. In winter, out-door games were Fox and Geese, snow fort battles, sledding, and ice skating on nearby ponds (Thomas 88). For shinny, a game similar to hockey, children used tree branches and wooden balls (Good 216-217). Staying indoors in bad weather saved the time of putting on and removing wet wraps. Rainy-day indoor games were Charades; Upset the Fruit Basket; Button, Button, Who's Got the Button? and Poor Pussy.

Spelling was typically the last subject of the day. The teacher tried to think of interesting ways to practice words. Spelldowns were a weekly event, and there were fierce contests between students. Spelling competitions with other school districts took place in the evening. The most commonly-used book was Noah Webster's *Elementary Spelling Book*, known as the Blue-Backed Speller. Learning to pronounce and spell words, called orthography, was more important than learning definitions. In later years, additional subjects like agriculture, home geography (science),

and composition were added. The subjects of physiology and hygiene did not emerge until almost 1900. When they did, the study was directed toward the evils of alcohol and smoking (Gulliford 56).

The school day ended at four o'clock with announcements from the teacher. Students had jobs assigned to them such as cleaning slates, putting away books, and sweeping the floor (Kline 25). Dismissed by rows, only students who misbehaved remained behind. Because of the rigorous school day and farm chores awaiting them at home, the teacher rarely assigned the children homework. However, students could earn home credits for doing tasks such as milking a cow, getting a meal, bathing, or going to bed early. This

A little roughhousing took place at this recess in the snow.

Interior of the Knisely School in Bedford County, Pennsylvania, shows the inside furnishings and floor arrangement of a late 1800s and early 1900s classroom.

encouraged good health practices and responsibility (Apps 18-19).

Even in the frame and brick school era, a teacher's duties did not begin and end with the academic lessons. Typical end-of-the-day chores included filling the crock with fresh water from the outside well, cleaning the blackboard, raking down the fire in the stove, emptying the coal bucket, dusting the windowsills and benches, checking the outhouses, and refilling the bucket at the coal house. Then, the teacher was ready to begin grading papers and planning the next day's lessons. When she could finally leave, she securely locked the doors and windows and walked home.

Students often had the responsibility of filling the coal bucket kept beside the pot-bellied stove.

Furnishing the Classroom

An upright metal stove dominated the center of most frame and brick one-room schools. Typically, the stove was the large, black pot-bellied style with a long, jointed stovepipe stretching across the ceiling. At other times, the iron stove stood at the front or back of the classroom (Fuller 35). The stove sat on cast iron legs with a metal pad or sand underneath. Due to the wooden floor and students seated nearby, flying sparks from the stove created a safety hazard. The amount of heat could not be regulated or evenly distributed. In winter, stuffy air near the stove stifled students while children near the outer walls shivered (Good 205-206).

A long black stovepipe ran the length of the rudely finished room, And a coal-oil lamp on a swinging chain helped dispel the gloom.
Helen Middleton

A coal bucket or wood bin sat close to the stove. In the schoolyard outside, a woodshed or coal house held a larger supply of fuel. At first, fuel was furnished by the families of students. Later, wood or coal was funded by the school directors who hired out a contract. In desperate times, twists of hay and cow piles could be utilized as sources of heat.

Mounted on the wall across the entire front of the room was a blackboard. Early blackboards were plain pine

This brick school shows many features such as the centrally-located iron stove, rows of wooden desks nailed to the floor, a raised platform, and a slate board across the front of the room. The school was moved from a nearby location to Swiss Heritage Village outside Berne, Indiana.

An Amish schoolhouse in Holmes County, Ohio, has a fresh supply of firewod in its lean-to woodshed.

boards which had been painted black. They needed to be repainted frequently. Slate boards were not widely used until the early 1900s. Erasers were either rags or sheepskin glued to wood blocks. The teacher wrote on the board with lumps of chalk called crayons (Gulliford 192). Foot benches on the floor made it possible for smaller children to reach the board when writing on it (Rosevink 160).

The teacher's desk was a four-legged oak table. A raised shelf on top held important materials like the class register, the handbell, and a few books. The desk stood in front of the room on a platform six to eight inches higher than the rest of the floor. This platform helped the teacher maintain authority. Because of the inconvenience of constantly stepping up and down, the platform floor design was later abandoned.

Tables pegged to the inside walls were eventually replaced with home-made, double-seated desks arranged in long rows. Students sat in pairs to assist each other. Boys sat on one side of the room while girls sat on the other.

By 1870, homemade desks had been discarded in favor of individual manufactured desks (Fuller 32). These desks could be ordered in various sizes to comfortably seat the smallest to the largest pupils from ages five to twenty. First graders usually sat in the front of the classroom behind the long recitation bench. Larger desks in back held children in the upper grades (Thomas 85).

These popular wooden desks were attached to sturdy iron legs. The desk-top had a fold-up bench attached to the front. When placed in rows, each bench provided a seat for the desk in front of it. The whole row of desks was nailed to the floor through long narrow planks.

Near the top of the slanted desk-top was a groove to hold pens and pencils. A small, round hole on one side fit around a glass or ceramic ink bottle.

A four-legged table on a raised platform in front of the classroom served as the teacher's desk. A large metal handbell sat prominently on top. Raised platforms were seldom used after the late 1800s.

Students often sat in pairs at double wooden desks. Girls sat on one side of the room and boys on the other. This 1850s school is from Kosciusko County, Indiana.

Underneath the desktop, a shelf held supplies such as a framed slate board, slate pencils, pencil boxes, homemade copybooks, felt erasers, and textbooks.

By the 1890s, the schools which had previously relied on natural lighting were furnished with kerosene lamps. The lamps were designed with reflectors, and they either extended from brackets in the wall or hung from the ceiling. Near the same time, window shades first appeared (Fuller 32-33).

Early classroom equipment included globes and pull-down maps, wall charts, and a few appropriate wall pictures. Rounding out the classroom furnishings were an unabridged dictionary on a stand, a pump organ, and a pendulum clock. The wall clock was enclosed in a wooden case with a glass window. A circle of black Roman numerals stood out on the clock face.

Few libraries existed before 1890. The county office prepared book boxes with material for all grade levels and rotated the boxes between schools (Webb 21). The first in-school library was perhaps a row of books on an open shelf. Later, a bookcase along the wall held fifty to sixty books. When standardized texts were

Typical one-room school furnishings by the 1890s were pendulum clocks, kerosene lamps, wall charts, and pump organs.

adopted, the school board assessed families of students a book fee. After using the books, some students passed them on to younger brothers and sisters.

School wells were dug on the school lot to provide an onsite water supply. Earlier schools would have

Kragera School, north of Becker, Minnesota, has recently been painted. The school is the current meeting place for the Kangaroo 4-H Club. A woodshed behind the school has an outhouse attached to both ends.

gotten their water from a nearby spring or farmhouse. Iron pump handles, often black in color, stood over the well close to the school. Before hygiene was understood, students drank from a common cup by dipping it into a pail or water crock which had been carried into the classroom. In warm weather, students drank directly from the pump. Later, children brought their own collapsible tin cups to school.

An iron pump handle still stands beside the Kragera School.

An 1890 frame schoolhouse is part of the Sauder Farm and Craft Village near Archbold, Ohio. Retired teachers in period dress share information with visitors about early schools inside the authentically-restored classroom. Originally in Michigan, Rose Hill School was used from 1890 to 1916.

The roof of the wide front porch hangs over two entrances to the frame school at Sauder Village. This allowed boys and girls to enter the school-room separately.

Extended School Year Stresses Academics

The length of the school year gradually extended from a winter and a summer term to an eight-month school year. The school began in September and ended in April. During this schedule, there was little vacation except a week off between Christmas and New Year's Day.

In 1921, Ohio's Legislature passed the "Bing Law." This law lengthened the school year to 180 days, or thirty-six weeks. Finally, students from the ages of six to eighteen were required to attend a full school year. However, if a student passed the seventh grade or was incapable of learning, he could be released at age sixteen (Thomas 21).

Ever since 1892. Ohio eighth grade students have taken examinations to test the proficiency in various subjects. This test, once called the Boxwell Exam, was developed by John Boxwell who later served as a state representative from Lima, Ohio (Sheeley 53). The results of the test, administered in April and May, determined whether or not country school students were ready to attend high school (Good 230). Passing grades were also necessary to graduate from eighth grade.

Questions for the Boxwell Exam were written by the State Commissioner of Common Schools and sent to the clerk of the county board. The test was given free of charge at a central location in each county. Subjects tested were orthography (spelling), arithmetic, writing, grammar, United States history, geography, and physiology (Sheeley 25-27).

Some sample questions in each subject reflect the years of memorization and rote learning which took place in one-room schools.

Orthography

1. Make and name the ordinary punctuation marks.
2. Give all the most important diacritical marks.
3. Give a list of four prefixes with their meanings and four suffixes with their meanings.

Arithmetic

1. From 100, subtract the sum of .371 and .0065; multiply the remainder by .3 and divide the product by .000005.
2. The proceeds of a 90-day note discounted at a bank at 6% 17 days after the date are $274.17. Find the face of the note.
3. What is the common denomination to which dry measure and liquid measure can be reduced? A cask that will contain ten bushels of wheat will contain how many gallons of water?

Writing

Copy the following in your best handwriting, giving care to punctuation and capitals:

Build thee more stately mansions,
   O my soul,
As the swift seasons roll!
Leave thy low-vaulted past!

Let each new temple nobler than
the last,
Shut thee from heaven with a
dome more vast,
Till thou at length art free,
Leaving thine outgrown shell by
life's unresting sea!

Grammar

1. Define analysis, synthesis, in-finitive, copula, and conjunc-tion.
2. Write two sentences, one of which shall contain an adjec-tive element of the third class, and the other an objective element of the third class.
3. Use in a sentence the posses-sive plural of son-in-law, a com-pound passive participle, and infinitive used adjectively and laid as a participle.

U.S. History

1. Name five of the original thir-teen colonies, with place and date of settlement of each.
2. Name five Union and five Confederate generals of the Civil War.
3. Give events connected with 1676, 1755, 1803, 1861, and 1876.

Geography

1. Bound West Virginia; give cap-ital and principal products.
2. Into what four classes are coral formations divided? Describe each.
3. What is a border sea? Give five examples.

Physiology

1. Describe the structure of muscles.
2. Trace fully the blood from the aorta to the vena cava.
3. Name the bones of the head.

The ability to answer the preced-ing questions would not be a useful life skill. The questions on the examination did not involve problem-solving. Many of these facts would be quickly forgotten several weeks later.

Chapter 8

School days, school days,
Good old Golden Rule days,
Reading and writing and 'rithmetic,
Taught to the tune of a hickory stick.

Discipline in Country Schools

Strict Rules Guide Students

According to a former one-room school teacher, "Families in the past set standards for their children, and children were trained from infancy to meet those standards" (Webb 15). One rule of discipline was, "If you got a spanking in school, you'd get two of them when you got home" (Webb 62). The small community surrounding the school was an extension of the family unit, and they helped set an example of behavior.

One main rule of the early classroom was to show respect for the teacher. Another important rule was not to disturb your neighbors while they were working. Students could leave their seats only with permission, and they were to move in and out of the classroom quietly (Rosevink 155). Because there

Seats attached to the desk of the classmate behind increased the temptation to misbehave.

Strict discipline rules helped a teacher maintain order in the classroom. Sitting on a dunce stool was an embarrassing and an uncomfortable punishment.

were so many lessons to teach, the one-room school teacher ran the classroom with strict rules.

Students may have been disciplined for many reasons. These included being late to school, giving wrong answers, throwing spitballs, chewing gum, whispering, slumping in their seats, or dropping marbles on the floor. There was the temptation to put a girl's long braids in the inkwell. Not finishing assignments was another main reason for punishment. And inevitably, older students picked on younger ones at recess or enroute to school.

Spanking was a primary form of discipline. Most former one-room school teachers mention that just displaying a paddle prevented many problems. However, when paddling was used, it was not a happy experience for the child. The child had to lean forward and grab his ankles while the teacher delivered the painful blows within hearing range of the class.

Other forms of punishment were not as severe, and the methods were as creative as the teacher using them. For

Schoolmarms did not always accompany their students outdoors for recess. They were kept busy planning lessons and organizing materials.

Playful spats took place in the schoolyard during recess. Older children kept younger brothers and sisters in line by telling on them when they got home.

disobeying, a student may have had to write a phrase on the board 100 times. Or, he had to memorize a long passage or copy and compute several pages of arithmetic problems to hand in.

Some punishments required physical endurance such as pointing a raised arm at a picture on the wall for an hour. Another was having a student place his nose on the board while standing on tiptoe. Or, the misbehaving child simply stood in a corner on a block of wood. The teacher sometimes hit the student's knuckles or open hand with the side of a wooden ruler. At other times, a student sat on a high stool wearing a dunce cap with a sign around his neck to explain the misdeed. Another punishment was to be seated very close or very far away from a hot stove.

There were yet more punishments handed out in the one-room school. Missing recess and staying after school were often used by the teacher. Then, the child might have had to sweep the classroom floor, clean the erasers, or carry out the trash for a week. Seating a mischievous boy beside a girl was also a punishment.

Usually, the classroom rule was that one student at a time could go to the outhouse. A student had to raise his hand and signal with one finger or two. This sign let the teacher know about how long a student would be gone (Kline 16-17). Some teachers used a system of "in" and "out" cards hung by the classroom door. If the cards were accidentally switched, a child waited a long time before going outside.

Even with all the punishments for breaking rules, students still thought up pranks, perhaps to break up the routine. Many pranks involved the outhouse, especially at Halloween. During the day, a little door on the back of the outhouse could be opened while someone was using the facility. This view provided

The outhouse, sometimes in disrepair, was a scheduled stop during the lunch hour and at recess. At other times, the teacher's permission was needed to make a visit.

an unusual target for snowballs in the winter. Frame outhouses could easily be moved from their foundations. Students relocated outhouses against the school door, out in a field, or in someone's front yard.

Another prank was smoking out the classroom. Older boys would climb to the school roof and plug the chimney by stuffing it with branches. Later, during the day, the trapped smoke filled the classroom, and everyone had to leave the room quickly! Sometimes, older boys would put buckshot inside the stove. When it eventually exploded, everyone in the classroom jumped in surprise!

During a lockout, students sneaked into the school before the teacher. They then kept the teacher locked out until she offered them a treat (Shinn 207).

The one-room school teacher had a difficult task to both educate and discipline her students. Discipline also was certainly a challenge, and some teachers quit their jobs mid-year in despair. No wonder a male teacher was sometimes necessary, especially when older farm boys attended. For without good discipline, not much learning could take place in the classroom.

An 1850s era schoolhouse stands on the grounds of Ohio Historical Village in Columbus, Ohio. The replica was the dream of members of the Ohio Retired Teachers Association who sponsored its construction in 1980.

Stringtown School in Jefferson Township, Williams County, 1898 — Front row, from left, John Knapp, Ivan Batterson, Ray Knapp, Alva Rittenower, John Mattoon, Alfred Opdycke; William Mattoon, Lucile Opdycke, Fay Knapp, Roy Knapp, John Finch; back row, Amos May, Bessie Opdycke, Bertha Knapp, Grace Rogers (teacher), Bernice Mattoon, Pearl

Stringtown School, District No. 7, 1898, located in Jefferson Township, Williams County, Ohio, with teacher Grace Rogers.

Chapter 9

Each Christmas we gave a program
Our parents and neighbors came to enjoy.
A pie and box supper was exciting
Hoping our box would be bought by that favorite boy.
Edna Cantrell

School / Community Events

Families Enjoy Social Life

School programs were big social events at the one-room schools. Parents and members of the community came to monthly programs at the school. Many programs related to holidays. No dancing or card parties were allowed. Some programs, arranged by the teacher, featured a speaker. The raised platform at one end of the schoolroom could be used as a stage area. Other schools improvised by hanging a sheet on a rope across the front of the room.

The interior of the Bridenbaugh School has been restored to its original condition. Built in 1878 and closed in 1928, the school served as a farm storage building before the current owner, Dale Bridenbaugh, undertook restoration. The school is located north of Pandora, Ohio.

Farver School, built in 1868, was recently restored as a community project and moved to the town of Shipshewana, Indiana. The frame building now serves as the town's public library.

The biggest event of the year was the Christmas program. To get ready, helpers moved desks to the side of the room so chairs could be set up. An overflowing crowd gathered to see the children act in a costumed play, recite memorized poems, and sing in duets and choruses. Afterwards, everyone ate bountiful refreshments.

At other times of the year, various fund-raisers helped offset school expenses. These usually involved food, such as box socials, pie socials, and penny socials. One country teacher remembers that kerosene lamps hung from trees in the schoolyard. Women and girls prepared fried chicken, potato salad, and pies. They placed the items in gaily-decorated boxes to be auctioned off to the highest bidder. The winner also claimed the prize of eating the meal with the female who had cooked the food.

For a pie social, ladies took great care in baking and wrapping their favorite kinds of pies. Even though the pies were not labeled on the outside, the pie bakers hid their names on the inside. Many young girls remember their beaus fiercely bidding for their pies and for the chance to sit with them and share each crusty morsel.

In contrast, at a penny social, everyone brought a dish of food to share. Food dishes were set on a long table. As each person took a serving, he paid a

These barefoot girls dressed up for a special day during the early 1920s in northern Ohio.

penny an item. The money raised from the event went into the school funds.

Field day was held at the end of the school year. Students and families from several schools in the same township got together. Everyone enjoyed various sport contests and outdoor games in addition to a huge picnic lunch at noon. Long tables were created by laying planks over the desktops (Good 227).

Sometimes, eighth grade graduations took place on the last day. Children spent the morning practicing recitations and songs in anticipation of an afternoon program. The teacher gave out treats, grade cards, and souvenir booklets. Souvenir booklets included the teacher's picture, a class list, names of school board members, and favorite poems (Rosevink 154). The county superintendent handed out diplomas to eighth graders.

Because of these many social events, the little schoolhouse down the road was already a familiar sight to young children. Even before reaching school age, youngsters had attended meetings and special programs there with their families. They had watched older brothers and sisters on their way to school. Family gatherings and community events revolved around the school. Everybody knew everyone else, and the children "had a sense of well-being and security" (Fuller 45).

One-room school instructors distributed souvenir booklets at the end of the school year. The booklet, intended as a memory of the year, contained a student roster, poems, the teacher's picture, and names of school board members. Walter Davis gave booklets to forty students at Rural Hall School in 1910.

Chapter 10

The modern schools are large and grand
and beautiful to see,
But how many love the country school
treasured in memory?
Helen Middleton

Consolidation of Schools
Country Schools vs. Urban Schools

At the turn of the century, sixteen million American children were being educated in one-room schools at country crossroads. Promoted by the state, but still controlled at the local level, these schools taught students the practical living skills and basic subjects to assimilate them into their rural environment. Only five percent of one-room school graduates went on to urban high schools.

In the 1890s and early 1900s, the country schools began to face criticisms from their urban counterparts. Urban educators said that one-room schools, run by local farmers, were behind the times. Critics pointed out the physical problems of poor heating, lack of electricity, and unclean outhouses, along with decaying buildings in the remote countryside. Critics claimed these conditions did not meet health and safety regula-

Consolidated schools at the turn of the century were larger, fancier structures which could accommodate each grade level in separate rooms. Many schools had two stories with classrooms, libraries, and gymnasiums.

This school building exemplifies improvements made by rural farmers to rectify criticisms. A white wooden fence surrounds the manicured school yard above.

tions. Other areas of concern included limited curriculum offerings, little competition among students, out-dated equipment, poorly trained teachers, inadequate places for play, and social isolation (Gulliford 118-119).

Urban schools were much different. Large, new urban school buildings had graded classrooms, indoor plumbing, electrical wiring, central heating systems, large gymnasiums, and well-stocked libraries. Around the year 1900, a Massachusetts educator, John Philbrick, is credited with designing a new concept. He created a school building with twelve equal-sized classrooms to house twelve separate grades, each grade with its own teacher. This design

was readily adopted by the urban school systems (Fuller 73-74).

"Consolidation of Schools" became the new educational phrase for the reform movement in education, reports Andrew Gulliford (119). By combining three or four country schools into one larger school, proponents of consolidation argued that a wider tax base could furnish better services and facilities for students. Larger school districts could provide more curriculum options, attract better teachers, and give students access to more up-to-date educational equipment.

But, experts had underestimated the dedication of farmers to their children's welfare. The farmers' response to these early criticisms of rural schools was to upgrade the condition of the existing one-room schools. School boards purchased maps and globes and more library books. They added playground equipment and built fences around the school yards. The wells and outhouses were upgraded and cleaned. Shutters, bell towers, and anterooms were added to the school buildings. Wayne Fuller suggests that courses such as nature study and agriculture became part of the curriculum to encourage students to stay in the country (46). Oftentimes, brand new one-room schools were built.

In a speech at the 1903 National Education Association Convention, the State Superintendent of Nebraska Schools spoke about the issue of conso-

An ornate bell tower graces the top of a brick schoolhouse.

lidation. He listed twice as many arguments for consolidation as opposing it. Some of his supporting statements were:

1. Pupils can be better classified and graded.

2. Pupils can have the advantage of better school rooms, better heated, better ventilated, and better supplied with apparatus.

3. Pupils have the advantage of that interest and enthusiasm and confidence which large classes bring.

Since community life in the country centered around the one-room schools, closing the school would affect the entire community. Some state legislatures passed measures to financially encourage farmers to consolidate several township schools. Certain areas of Ohio and Indiana were among the first to consolidate rural school districts. But, few other midwestern states followed. Most farmers still opposed consolidation as a plot by state legislators and educators to take away their control of the schools (Fuller 97-100). After all, the one-room schools had identified their communities and provided a stable environment to raise their families for over a century.

For the first time, in 1920, more Americans were living in towns than in the country. The urban population had a certain disdain for rural farmers and their backward ideas. This period of urban growth and reform was short-lived because of the ensuing financial crisis in our country.

This frame school in Holmes County, Ohio, known as Wise School, closed its doors in 1959. Students then moved to a new, four-room brick building next door. The south side of the school has a full row of tall windows. The north, tree-shaded side has none. This feature was once thought to make the best use of natural lighting. The school has a full basement.

The white frame school above stands beside a modern brick elementary building in Intercourse, Pennsylvania. This structure is now used as a public library.

During the Depression years of the 1930s, many Americans returned to their rural roots in order to survive. The stability of midwestern farm life and the courage of its people once again held appeal. Independence and resourcefulness became desirable traits.

At this time, Fuller concludes that there was not much incentive to give up the one-room schools which had served them well (109). Troubled times did sometimes force farmers to reduce teachers' salaries or shorten the school year. But, during the Depression, the one-room schoolhouse remained the symbol of continuity and hope for the future. Social lives still centered around school programs and PTA meetings. In the bleakest days, federal funds even kept the one-room schools in operation.

The late 1800s and early 1900s brought great waves of immigrants to America. The midwestern schools were challenged to teach immigrant children about the American culture. Since the state required immigrant children to attend English-speaking schools, rural schools played an important role in this task.

German immigrants could own land for the first time, and they could practice their religion freely. In the late 1800s, over 180,000 Mennonites made their home in the Midwest. At first, they organized their own German-speaking schools. Gradually, they became part of the English-speaking schools (Gulliford 93). Still, many large

This Amish school, hidden in a farm yard, is located in Lancaster County, Pennsylvania. Such plain stone structures appear about every mile in Amish neighborhoods. Below, the Amish classroom still resembles the floor plan and instructional methods used in early one-room schools with the raised platform and the old-style desks.

The Snake Hill School, also known as Maple Grove School, from Leacock Township in Lancaster County, Pennsylvania, is now located at the Landis Valley Museum where visitors enjoy seeing the restored structure.

families kept their children home to work. Often the family's livelihood depended on the oldest child helping with chores.

Today in Pennsylvania, as in other midwestern Amish settlements, Amish one-room schools educate students in grades one through eight. Until consolidation, Amish children attended one-room schools. Because of consolidation, Amish farmers decided to separate their children from the schools in town. As the empty one-room schools were placed on the auction block, the Amish purchased them. They also built additional schoolhouses to continue the tradition of educating their children in the rural environment.

In Lancaster County, Pennsylvania, alone, there are currently 153 Old Order Amish and Old Order Mennonite Schools (Klimuska 7). After a hard-fought legal battle from 1937 to 1972, the Amish were granted permission to educate their children separately and end their formal schooling after the eighth grade (Lapp 555). With no further education, the Amish expect their offspring to pursue practical occupations which will benefit their own community.

Consolidation Proceeds Slowly

Wayne E. Fuller said that in 1936, following thirty years of reform movements in the Midwest, nearly 70,000

This two-room school, north of Syracuse, Indiana, was known as Hex School. It is now used as a private school. Below is the student body of a neighboring two-room school in Elkhart County, Indiana, in the year 1924. Built identical to the one above, it was called Juday School. The instructor, Miss Musselman, stands in the center of the back row among her charges.

These two former one-room schoolhouses have been remodeled into homes in the country. The one above, in Vistula, Indiana, has had few exterior changes. The red-brick structure below, which is in Defiance County in northwest Ohio, has several additions. Located at the corner of Domersville and Jewell Roads, it was known as Prosser School.

one-room schools still dotted the countryside. Almost sixty percent of schools in the old Northwest Territory had one room. In the seven other midwestern states, nearly eighty percent of schools were one-room. There were only 4,000 consolidated schools, and many of these had only two rooms. Even with the advent of the automobile, midwestern farm children continued their mile or two-mile walk to school along country roads, much like the generations before them (105-108).

By the late 1930s, electricity had arrived at most one-room schools. The government assisted districts by inspecting school facilities and building sanitary outhouses. Most schools kept in touch with current events via radios. The moralistic lessons in *McGuffey Readers* were replaced with the new textbook series. New educational goals about social interaction and problem-solving were added to the curriculum. And, teacher training came under scrutiny.

By the beginning of World War II, despite the predominance of one-room schools, the Midwest had one of the highest rates of literacy in the country. Like no other previous event, World War II changed America. It uprooted people from their environments, altered the work force, changed the graphics of population, and upset family roles and structure.

After World War II, in the late 1940s, state legislatures passed laws to outline procedures for consolidation of schools. The laws established school boards to oversee the changes. At the county level, committees were allowed to make plans for reorganization. Then, a

referendum to vote on the county plans would be held.

Such a massive undertaking involved educating citizens at all levels, including the county committee members. Newly-paved roads and better transportation and communication made it difficult to argue against consolidation. Some counties, however, held up the process by refusing to select a committee or by having an inactive committee. Sometimes, voters rejected a committee's plan for reorganization (Fuller 119, 122).

Consolidation Affects Williams County, Ohio

About eighty years ago, in 1917, consolidation became a big issue in Williams County, Ohio. W.A. Salter, the first county superintendent, explained the advantages to rural school districts. Like other midwestern counties, the new idea held little appeal for the farmers. Since the late 1850s, they had been satisfied with the instruction their children had received in one-room schools. They felt no need to increase their tax burdens because of a new concept about schools.

The eastern part of the county in Madison, Brady, and Millcreek Townships was the first area to act. The village of Kunkle established a centralized high school about 1920, soon followed by Stryker, West Unity, and Pioneer. Before consolidation began, only about sixty percent of rural students in Williams County were going on to graduate from high school (Thomas 92-93). The county seat of Bryan had

The village of West Unity built one of the first consolidated high schools in Williams County, Ohio, in 1921. Bricks from some former one-room schools were used for the inside walls. The main building still stands today, and additions have been added.

educated some of these students, having operated its high school since the 1870s (Cooley and Maynard 37). In West Unity, rural schoolchildren were transported to the consolidated school in horse-drawn school buses. Five routes were needed to carry students from parts of three surrounding townships.

Even today, in the eastern part of Williams County, very few remnants of one-room schools exist. Interestingly, several brick schools in Brady Township were torn down about the same time, including Smitley, Lantz, and Hamer. Mary Hutchinson Thomas wrote that their bricks were then used to build the

School consolidation in Pioneer, Ohio, required one of the first horse-drawn school buses before the days of motorized buses (1919). The distances from outlying areas were now too great for pupils to walk.

inner walls of the new 1921 West Unity High School (75).

Throughout the county, the building of new centralized schools and the closing of one-room schools was a slow process which spanned nearly forty years, from 1920 to 1957. Not all one-room schools closed at the same time, even in the same township. Some closings were necessitated by dwindling school populations. For a number of years, country schools still served elementary children, but it became more common for a larger percentage of rural eighth grade graduates to attend high school in nearby towns. Finally, the *Northwest Historian* reports that the Williams County School Board officially closed all one-room schools in 1957 (WCHS).

The consolidation movement, or reorganization, took local politics out of schools. Centralized high schools, middle schools, and grade schools were built in towns. They were divided into grade levels like urban school systems, and principals were hired to supervise the daily activities of students and staff.

With the end of the one-room school era, the empty school buildings either reverted back to the landowners, or they were offered for sale by the township at public auctions. Afterwards, some schools remained on the same sites. Some were moved elsewhere on skids and altered in form and use. A few were torn down to expand surrounding farm fields.

For example, the Bunker Hill School in Jefferson Township, which consolidated with West Unity in 1917, was sold in 1919 to S.S. Wineland for $40.

The wood shed brought $49 from Leland Starr. And another bidder paid $28 for the outhouse (Thomas 81). Of course, the purchasers were responsible themselves for moving the structures.

The first Beatty School in Brady Township was built in 1868. This log building was later moved to the George Beatty home and attached to the house. A new frame school was then constructed and used as a school until 1937. After consolidation, George Beatty II bought the building and used it for grain storage. After 1944, it was remodeled into a home by former students, William and Lucille Clark (Thomas 79). Further tenants remodeled the home again as recently as 1995.

Was consolidation an improvement? One former schoolteacher in Jefferson Township, Grace Geesey, taught for thirty-nine years, retiring in 1976. Her first sixteen years were at several one-room schools in Superior Township. Having studied in a one-room school herself as a child, Grace has vivid memories of her experiences.

Grace's largest class in a one-room school numbered fifty, which represented about twenty families. Usually, she taught about twenty pupils a year from nearby farms. Few of the children had ever traveled far from home. As the rural population decreased, the least number of students she had was twelve.

Grace mentioned the strong points of the one-room school. She said students truly cared about one another and worked cooperatively. Older children served as an example and helped discipline younger ones. There was more truth-telling because brothers and sisters tattled on each other at home. Religion was a strong part of their lives, and parents were supportive of the school.

When country schools in Superior Township closed in 1952, the new Superior School south of Montpelier provided a centralized location. The new building had four classrooms with two grades housed in each room. Fewer teachers were needed in the township, so some teachers were out of a job. Grace said that during the first year of consolidation, she had fifty third and fourth graders in one room. Though they were crowded, students now had the advantage of a hot lunch program, indoor plumbing, and central heating. Other changes required a transition period for the teachers and students.

Mykrantz Normal Academy, operated by C.W. Mykrantz in the 1860s and 1870s, was a privately-owned Normal School, or training institution for teachers in Bryan, Ohio. When the public schools became too crowded, the building was bought by the local school board.

Many Williams County, Ohio, teachers attended the August Teachers' Institute held in Bryan, Ohio, in 1909.

Chapter 11

Speak gently; it is better far
To rule by love than fear;
Speak gently; let no harsh words mar
The good we might do here.
George Langford

Certification of Teachers

Requirements Continue to Change

Teacher certification was a simpler matter in the days of one-room schools. The earliest teachers were qualified after completing eight grades and passing the eighth-grade test. An applicant was merely questioned by the local school board who okayed the certification. Most teachers were quite young when they began their careers. In Williams County, married women were not hired until the 1930s, and then only rarely. It was felt that an unmarried teacher could concentrate better on her duties.

In 1880, the state of Ohio required teacher certification, and soon each candidate took a written examination in order to secure a certificate. Educational leader, Horace Mann, was instrumental in founding a system of teacher-training schools. By the early 1900s, teachers had to attend college at a Normal School, a training institution specifically for teachers. Some were privately run, such as Fayette Normal School, begun in 1882, and the Mykrantz Normal Academy in Bryan, which operated in the 1860s and 1870s. Soon, Ohio established

state-run Normal Schools in places such as Bowling Green and Kent. At first, teachers could obtain a one-year teaching certificate with twenty-four weeks of training. Then, coursework was extended to a year. Subsequent certificates were issued to teachers who passed examinations or took additional summer sessions.

Written examinations given to potential teachers were long and complicated. Elementary teachers were tested in ten subject areas including orthography, English grammar, writing, U.S. history, reading, theory and practice, geography, literature, arithmetic, and physiology and narcotics. High school teachers were also tested on their knowledge of geometry, algebra, physical geography, botany, physics, bookkeeping, Latin, civil government, Germany, general history, and rhetoric (Thomas 39-40).

The practice of a two-year Normal School teaching degree became obsolete in the 1960s. By the end of that decade, all new Ohio public schoolteachers were required to complete a four-year college

A one-room brick school on Penn Grant Road in Lancaster County, Pennsylvania, was first remodeled into a home. Later, it housed a craft store.

degree in their specific field. Elementary teachers had to acquire a bachelor's degree in education which included a certain number of hours in various subject areas and a supervised practice teaching experience. Being a high school teacher also required a four-year degree with special emphasis on the subject area to be taught.

After completing a college degree, a potential teacher filed an application and his college transcripts with the State Department of Education. After review, the State Department issued a provisional four-year teaching certificate. The certificate specified grade levels and/or subject areas to be taught. A teacher could then periodically renew his certificate based on successful teaching and

completion of additional coursework. If enough courses or a master's degree was obtained, an active teacher could apply for a professional or permanent teaching certificate.

Over the years, the State Department of Education and the Ohio General Assembly have sought ways to improve instruction. The latest change has been a shift from issuing teaching certificates to licensing teachers. Preparation requirements for new elementary teachers will include additional coursework in the teaching of reading and phonics. New teachers in Ohio will undergo a two-year entry level period on their provisional licenses. They must renew their licenses every five years with additional coursework. By the year 2003, newly-licensed Ohio teachers must acquire a master's degree to continue teaching beyond ten years (Legislative Update).

An Educational Task Force of Ohio teachers strongly suggests that teachers be prepared and certified in their teaching assignment areas. In the past, because of teacher shortages, teachers were sometimes hired out of their fields. This is seldom a factor now, though it is harder to find qualified math and science teachers at the secondary level.

During the late 1800s, a teacher's salary was about a dollar a day. Then, by 1912, salaries gradually increased to $40 a month. When the first county schools consolidated, salaries increased to $60 to $70 a month (Rosevink 156). Until the 1950s, men were paid more than women, even for doing the same teaching job. In society, men were considered the main support for their families. At the same time, high school teachers were paid more than elementary teachers.

In the past, the one-room country schoolteacher was isolated with her charges. Once in a while, the county superintendent would stop by in the fall and in the spring to inspect how things were going. According to Grace Geesey, there was no formal evaluation of teachers. However, an informal evaluation by the surrounding community was ongoing, because the teacher was expected to

This former schoolhouse in northern Lancaster County has been remodeled into a picturesque home.

Banner Oak School, located near Temperance, Michigan, was built by a Toledo architect, Fred Ludwig, in 1871. Classes last used the school in 1955 before they consolidated with Bedford Public Schools.

do her duty and to behave properly. To prevent problems, the county superintendent rotated teachers from school to school around the township.

With the development of consolidated school districts, schools now had supervisors called principals. The principal was available to make a more formal evaluation of a teacher's effectiveness in the classroom. At first, this was like a written narrative, based on an observation in the classroom. Evaluations today may also include checklists and goals to be obtained. Usually, teachers with less experience are observed more frequently and advised by superiors. Thus, mutual goals can be agreed upon, and the teacher can work toward these aims.

The Ohio State Board of Education has issued new standards for teacher training both before teachers begin teaching and throughout their careers. The new standards apply not only to teachers, but to other school personnel including counselors, principals, and superintendents. Each school district designs a broad range of ongoing professional development opportunities for staff members. Beginning teachers receive coaching and mentoring from experienced classroom teachers. Educational service centers, formerly known as county offices of education, provide

The brick school above stands on privately-owned land at the edge of Alexandria, Ohio, in Licking County.

professional growth opportunities for educators. Specialized leadership academies provide training for team-building, school-based management, and strategic planning for improvement of schools (Voinovich).

Chapter 12

If you would have your learning stay
Be patient—don't learn too fast:
The man who travels a mile each day
May get round the world at last.
McGuffey's Third Reader

Curriculum and Instruction
Role of School Expands

A primary reason for consolidation of schools was to provide a more competitive classroom environment. Students could be exposed to better instruction and newer educational materials. Though teachers in one-room schools worked hard, their time to assist individuals was limited. Students spent much time on independent work, waiting for the teacher to call them forward. Teachers made few provisions for student learning styles or higher-level thinking skills. It was a challenge just to get through all the subjects for various grade levels.

With consolidation of schools, new buildings were divided into separate classrooms, each occupied by one or two different grade levels. A teacher could devote her energies to the lessons and needs unique to her group. An elementary teacher still taught many subjects,

The 1870 brick school at Reads Landing in Minnesota was once part of a thriving Mississippi River town. All four classrooms helped educate students up through high school until 1957. The Wabasha County Historical Society has displayed artifacts there since acquiring the school in 1965.

The former Buttles School, District No. 4, north of Waterford, Wisconsin, once educated rural students. The school is now a private residence.

but she could track student progress and offer more timely help.

Each class was now part of a student body led by a principal. Sometimes, one adult doubled as both teacher and principal. Instead of being isolated, classroom teachers were now supported by other staff members. Besides regular teachers, special instructors for music, art, and physical education were employed. Today, staff members might also include areas such as guidance counselors, school psychologists, school nurses, reading specialists, tutors, librarians, speech therapists, computer coordinators, and curriculum directors. Non-certified personnel such as custodians, secretaries, and teacher aides are also vital.

One-room school classrooms were starkly furnished and rigidly arranged. Instruction was piecemeal in short time slots. The student body was composed of children from only a few families. The teacher alone handled daily instruction. Decisions regarding maintenance and paying bills were made by the local school board. Parents wholeheartedly supported the teacher's efforts.

Today, subjects are not separated into short time periods. But, even through the 1980s, the state required classroom teachers to plan schedules which included so many minutes of each subject. Middle schools and high schools often use the bell system to divide the day into seven or eight equal time periods. While this is a method of

A little red schoolhouse adds to the historic charm of downtown Tomah, Wisconsin. Moved from a rural location, the building, known as Water Mill School, stands in Gilett Park on Main Street. Originally painted white, it was used as a school from 1865 to 1963.

The interior of the Water Mill School features an entry room. The small-sized school has four short rows of desks and a recitation bench in front of the teacher's desk.

A hewn, log school first stood on this site in Walled Lake, Michigan. Stonecrest School, shown here, was built of native stone laid in quicklime mortar in 1860. Located on the highest point of the original village, the school now serves the Commerce Township Area Historical Society.

Walled Lake Middle School stands just a couple miles west of Stonecrest School. Its size and architecture illustrate how the needs of school buildings have changed.

organization, it has not been proven to enhance learning. A more recent practice is the move toward integration of subjects. By overlapping subject areas in meaningful relationships, students experience more relevance to actual life.

Today, there is more emphasis placed on the overall learning environment. Schools still need the encouragement and support of parents. To maximize learning, schools also benefit by combining efforts with businesses, lawmakers, the community, and society as a whole.

Changes in today's society make learning goals more difficult to achieve. Problems in families have caused shifts in the role of schools. Student populations are now more diverse in many ways, and students present wide differences in academic abilities and instructional needs. Changes in the work force and economy have altered expectations about what students should know. School curriculums have been affected by the rapid expansion of information and technology (OEA Reform 1-3).

Besides the academic subjects that were stressed in one-room schools, today's educators are challenged to develop life-long learners who are aware of global issues. The ability to find and use information and to think critically takes precedence over memorization of facts. Developing time-management skills and self-discipline become aims for students of today. The importance of communication skills, which include interacting cooperatively with others, is emphasized, even in the primary grades.

Educators today recognize the developmental stages of children. Teachers plan a broad range of activities appropriate for the interests and needs of each age level. As students mature, they learn to apply skills while they focus on experiences in specific areas. Intermediate-age children participate in discussions and problem-solving, and they actually experience democracy in action. Middle school students participate in a balanced, inter-disciplinary curriculum which takes into account their unique changes. And, high school students choose from a wide range of electives to maintain their interests while they explore the humanities, fine arts, and career opportunities (OEA Task Force).

School Responds to Special Needs Students

Since passage of the federal law in 1975 to insure the education of all handicapped children to their highest potential, many states have spent large amounts of money for special programs. The criteria for identifying special students and the process of meeting their needs have gone through many changes. The labels applied to programs have changed almost as often.

Terms first used for developmental handicaps were "Trainable Mentally Retarded" and "Educable Mentally Retarded." The EMR students were housed in regular schools, but they were taught in separate classrooms known as "Special Education." Then, the label, "Developmentally Handicapped" (DH), was used for these students.

Dewey School served as Waterloo Township's District No. 15 from 1844 to 1963. Located south of Stockbridge, Michigan, on Territorial Road, the school is now part of a rural museum.

Being "Learning Disabled" (LD) became a catch-all phrase for many conditions which caused learning problems. Recognized disabilities include autism, hearing handicaps, orthopedic and physical handicaps, speech and language handicaps, visual handicaps, and traumatic brain injuries (Annual Report 5). Some students display "Severe Behavior Handicaps" (SBH) involving their social and emotional behavior. Now, most handicapped children are referred to as "Special Needs Students." Two increasingly common disorders, "Attention Deficit Disorder" (ADD) and "Attention Deficit Hyperactivity Disorder" (ADHD), can prevent students from being able to

focus and achieve in the classroom. According to experts, ADHD occurs in four to seven percent of all children. Such difficulty causes learning and social problems at home and school (Kopf). Underlying causes for ADD or ADHD can be exposure to drugs and alcohol prenatally, premature birth, poor diet, food allergies, and chemical imbalances in the brain.

In Ohio, more severely handicapped children were once educated in separate schools. Since building such schools had to be approved by voters, similar facilities were not built across the state. Higher achieving handicapped children attended separate classes in the regular school taught by specially-trained teachers. Later, these handicapped students were "mainstreamed" into regular classes for activities such as gym and music and in academic areas when they were capable. Ramps and elevators were installed to make school buildings more accessible.

The most recent trend for educating the handicapped has been "Inclusion." Handicapped students are placed in the regular classroom, the least restrictive environment, and the special-education teacher becomes a resource person. While she still writes Individual Education Plans (IEPs) for her students, she joins the classroom teacher to provide academic assistance (OEA Reform 12-13). The handicapped student is among his peers, and the special teacher is present to help. Some students can be assigned "504" status, which means they cannot be discriminated against because of their handicap when given grades and tests.

Most schools in Ohio and the nation receive Title I funds to assist students who have trouble keeping up academically with their classmates. Title I can finance special reading and math classes and individual tutoring such as Reading Recovery programs.

The purpose of Improving America's Schools Act of 1994, or Title VI, was to promote innovative improvements and programs. These are geared toward students with special educational needs and the at-risk students. Funds may also be used to hire learning disability tutors and teachers (Annual Report 5).

A bell tower gives evidence that this home once served as a rural schoolhouse in northern Michigan.

Programs for gifted students are also included under the designation of special education by the state. These programs have not been as readily funded as programs for low-achievers. There was the general belief that students with high-level abilities could get along without extra help.

More recently, the unique characteristics and concerns of gifted children have been recognized, and more state funding has been provided. For awhile, separate classes and pull-out programs were provided for the gifted. But now, gifted students are usually part of the regular classroom, with the classroom teacher challenging them beyond the regular curriculum. Labels for gifted students have also gone through changes such as GT (Gifted and Talented) and TAG (Talented and Gifted). The practice today is to identify gifted and high-achieving students at all grade levels and in various areas such as academic, creativity, music, art, athletics, and drama.

In the days of one-room schools, the special needs of handicapped students were either undiagnosed or largely ignored. Other than making minor adjustments, teachers had neither the time nor the finances to deal with such problems. Because schools today assume the responsibility of educating all types of children, meeting the needs of handicapped students becomes a more important priority. Ohio school districts now attempt to locate and evaluate all children with disabilities from birth to age twenty-one (Annual Report 5). Infant and preschool programs provide early intervention for children with delayed developments.

Teachers Seek Ways To Reach Goals

One-room school teachers and today's teachers have both faced lack of time to teach and inadequate time to plan lessons and evaluate student progress. For many reasons, there is not enough direct contact time with students. Most students today are preoccupied rather than giving their full attention in class.

Teachers must begin many tasks after students have departed for the day. These jobs include planning for instruction, selecting materials and equipment, grading student work, and planning for assessments. Teachers must collaborate with other staff members and confer with parents. Teachers can easily become bogged down with non-instructional duties.

A problem unheard of in country schools was keeping up with technology. The global economy, computer literacy, the Internet, and the World Wide Web were not previously factors of concern. Today, using the computer to network for learning resources is an objective. Computers can be useful educationally for writing reports, sharing information, and keeping records.

Advances in computer technology take place faster than new computers can be installed. Most schools have computer labs, especially in the upper grades. State grants have helped equip schools with computers. The state of Ohio has recently proposed that its schools have a student/computer ratio of five to one. Much of the installation involves rewiring old school buildings

The Oswegoland Heritage Association oversees the historic Little White School Museum in Oswego, Illinois. Built in 1854 in Greek Revival style, it is the town's oldest public building. The stately school now houses a historical museum.

which were constructed before the computer age.

In days of one-room schools, the local school board selected and paid for textbooks. Later, county school offices recommended basic texts to cover curriculum. More recently, local curriculum committees, composed of teachers and a director of curriculum, have designed studies for their subject areas. Proposed curriculums are sent to the state for approval. Afterwards, the school board, upon the Superintendent's recommendation, adopts the curriculum and a particular series of textbooks. Not all county school districts adopt the same books.

Presently, the State Department of Education in Ohio has developed a state-wide competency-based curriculum model for various subjects. Local school district curriculums must complement and expand these models in order to provide instruction and assessment in the classroom. In the early 1990s, Ohio's State Department of Education mandated that students in grades four, six, nine, and twelve take the state-developed Proficiency Tests.

Teaching methods have changed over the years. Movements in education seem to occur in cycles, and the pendulum swings back and forth. Sometimes,

This 1886 Pleasant Township, Indiana, schoolhouse now houses services for a Presbyterian Church. First abandoned in the 1930s, it was used as a farm storage building. In 1974, the school was restored to serve summer worshipers from nearby lakes. Even though a new church stands next door, the old school still hosts the 11:00 a.m. service.

a new trend is merely an old idea which has been renamed. Some methods of instruction in recent decades have been the open classroom, learning stations, individualized instruction, team teaching, departmentalized instruction, ability grouping, cooperative learning, multi-age grouping, peer teaching, inclusion, and block scheduling, to name a few. Parts of each method have merit. Some practices, such as individualized instruction, multi-age grouping, and peer teaching were already in place in the one-room schools.

Today, trends in teaching methods continue to change. There is the trend toward less teacher-directed instruction and more inductive learning. Instead of reading basal texts, students choose from a wide variety of original books. More in-depth time is devoted to fewer topics. Attention is given to varied learning styles, and students are given more responsibility for completing their own goals. Even John Dewey, an educational reformer in the early 1900s, emphasized the value of learning through a variety of activities. He believed learning should be an active experience (Merrow Report).

Hicks School has stood on a corner east of Pinckney, Michigan, since 1849. The frame school was closed in 1972. In a community project, the school was restored in 1984.

Gosswiller School is part of Long Grove's historical village in Illinois. The red school-house now houses a popular chocolate shop downstairs and a French specialty shop on the first floor. The school was one of four schools located in Long Grove in 1880.

In 1910, a new brick school with an entryway and bell tower replaced an older two-story frame school in Briceton, Ohio.

Chapter 13

Never will a machine or
a fine building replace
a human being as a teacher.
Jerry Apps

Facilities and Equipment
Adaptations Match Demands and Funding

In the early days, the main materials for teaching were textbooks, though limited in number, a dictionary, and slate boards. Later, reference books, maps and globes, and wall charts were added by some foresighted school boards. The earliest texts had to be purchased by the students themselves. By the 1900s, most school boards furnished their district's textbooks for various subjects. Each school board had only to concern itself with maintaining the roof, walls, and foundation of a one-room building. Even so, the structure was sometimes sadly neglected.

The responsibility of providing adequate school facilities to carry out educational goals in the information age is much more demanding. Equipping classrooms and special areas with materials for a diverse group of learners is complicated. The floor plan in today's school must be adapted to the latest mandates in curriculum and instruction. Besides classrooms, numerous other room areas for a variety of educational activities are needed. Providing accessibility for all students is also a concern.

In order to protect the physical well-being of students, there must be a well-maintained structure. Many aids to good health such as adequate restrooms, water coolers, and heating and cooling systems with proper ventilation are a necessity. Natural and artificial lighting and safe floors add to the comfort of students (OEA Task Force). School-wide warning systems for tornadoes, fires, and earthquakes are required by law.

Many kinds of spaces are needed by students and teachers throughout the day. Important activity areas for students are a library, a small theater with a stage, an art studio, health facilities such as exercise areas, food courts with creative seating arrangements, separate areas equipped for music, computer areas throughout the school, and smaller spaces for special classes such as speech or guidance. Teachers need teacher planning and preparation areas, conference rooms, work areas, storage space, resource centers, and separate teacher lounges. The school design needs to be comfortable and inviting with small nooks and clusters of learning areas (Sabo 11-15).

In the 1940s, when the armed services used audio-visual equipment to train soldiers, educators discovered new ways to utilize such equipment (Thomas 50). With audio-visuals, teachers involved children's senses and brought the outside world into the classroom. A battery-powered radio may have been one of the first links to the outside. Today, standard equipment includes not only filmstrip projectors, but wall-mounted, large-screen TVs, VCRs, record players and CDs, tape recorders, overhead projectors, video cameras, and production equipment. Communication between rooms is aided by public address systems. The computer Internet connects classrooms to the world beyond. Using such equipment increases the number of electric outlets, phone lines, and cable hook-ups which modern schools require.

The physical structure of modern school buildings must be adapted to varied learning situations. Teachers are no longer dispensers of information, but they act as facilitators of learning. Classrooms are arranged to provide freedom of movement, centers for activity and learning, display areas, and enclosed space for storage. Replacing standard classrooms are rooms of various sizes with movable walls. Tables are replacing desks so students have more opportunity to work together. Spaces need to be flexible in case several groups need to meet together for a presentation or just a few students are working as a small group (OEA Task Force).

An important factor for adequate school buildings and equipment is school funding. The funding of schools has been difficult for several reasons. Because of a declining birth rate and more older persons, there is a smaller proportion of the population which has school-age children. Older persons generally have limited income and less direct interest in school operations. The political environment has been more critical of schools. At the same time, legislatures have mandated programs without providing additional funding, or they have actually decreased funding for existing programs. The percentage of state general revenue funds for elementary and secondary education has been gradually reduced. These revenues have gone instead to help fund Corrections, Human Services, and Medicaid.

With the difficulty of passing school bond issues and operating levies and the unpredictability of state funding, school districts, especially in Ohio, must find creative ways of updating school buildings. Committees combining teachers and community members can study the best possibilities for using or converting existing structures. Sometimes, corporate contributions and community fund-raisers help the cause.

When building new structures, there are money-saving techniques. One method is to build several buildings on one plot of land so they can share common parking lots, athletic fields, and kitchens. Using a prototype design can cut down on architectural costs. Sharing school facilities with community groups keeps the community aware of maintaining quality buildings (Sabo 12).

Chapter 14

Families and Discipline
Role of School Alters

There is an old African proverb, "It takes a village to raise a child." This belief suggests that raising a child involves everyone in a community, not just parents. The concept is easier to picture in the confines of a small African village where a child grew up among an extended family of relatives who took special interest in training him in the ways of the village.

During the era of one-room schoolhouses in small crossroad villages, such

community support also existed. A child was a valued part of the family and community, and there were certain practices for his behavior and responsibilities. In familiar surroundings near grandparents, cousins, and neighbors, a child worked, played, and worshipped. This secure environment provided role models to reinforce the expectations of both parents and community members.

Today's village is much larger and more diverse. Even though the concept

In the countryside near Pepin, Wisconsin—birthplace of Laura Ingalls Wilder—stands a picturesque school setting. The brick schoolhouse and yard have been well-preserved as a home.

Sunnyview School, built in 1882, is part of the Chippewa Valley Museum at Carson Park in Eau Claire, Wisconsin. In use as a school until 1961, elementary students now visit it to experience pioneer education.

of a village has changed, there is still the human need for community. Such close support is now more difficult to achieve. Children live in towns and metropolitan areas, sometimes distant from the schools they attend. Grandparents may be hundreds of miles away and unable to be a regular part of their lives. The family unit has been altered because of both parents in the work force, single-parent families, and more exposure to different lifestyles and cultures.

What is a child's community today? Do parents encourage their children and try to provide positive guidance? H.J. Cummins writes in the *Minneapolis Star Tribune* that since the 1960s, the divorce rate has doubled, and the number of one-parent families has tripled. Nearly one in three babies is born to an unmarried mother. Parents often change their marital status without considering the impact of their actions on children.

Twenty percent of children in the United States live at the poverty level, meaning income for a family of four is less than $12,674. A recent study suggested that this problem affects twenty to twenty-four percent of Ohio's children. Women head ninety percent of single-parent homes, and they fall into poverty at some time during their lives (U.S. Census).

How do these poverty statistics affect a child's life? Children from impoverished homes are more likely to have poor health habits and do poorly in school. As adults, many become single parents themselves, they cannot hold jobs, and they frequently break the law.

Most parents spend an average of seventeen hours a week with their children. This includes the time they spend together in front of the television. Few families sit down to eat meals together. Since 1970, the percentage of moms who have jobs outside the home has risen from forty to seventy percent. Child care has been delegated to others, and even preschoolers spend much of their time in day care.

Parents with outside jobs have long work weeks and are given few vacations. Employers have demanded more and more from them while disregarding any family obligations they may have. The schedule of working full time and running a household which includes children is exhausting. This has limited the amount of time and the quality of guidance that children could once depend upon thirty or more years ago.

The *Minneapolis Star Tribune* recently pointed out that television and movies influence the lives of young children. They are watching long hours of inappropriate programming, often unsupervised. Shows with sexually explicit and violent material do little to help them cope socially and emotionally, and such situations are presented as norms

of behavior. Indeed, the increase in violence from street gangs to the school playground continues to grow. While murders have dropped in recent years, murders among teens have more than doubled. Teenage drug use and suicides have also risen. In fact, the fifteen largest school districts in the country list their three biggest problems as gangs, weapons, and drug use (Lieberman 39).

Many schools are not safe for either students or teachers. Long-term prevention programs are needed to provide safe environments that foster learning. Problems such as alcohol and drug abuse, violence, and teen suicide are so profound that communities can only develop solutions by working together at all levels. This involves assessing the problems and establishing firm policies. Ongoing training for school staff and parents is needed to implement prevention programs. Businesses and law enforcement agencies also need to

The Willow Lawn School can now be found at Galloway Village in Fond du Lac, Wisconsin. The frame structure, once located on Hickory Road southwest of the city, was last used as a school in 1963.

This stone school near Jonesville, Michigan, has been well-preserved. Located at a crossroad beside U.S. Route 12, the school, known as Bretty School, is now a privately-operated craft store.

This ca1880 frame building was a schoolhouse west of Luray, Virginia, until the late 1930s. Known as Massanutten School, it became the property of the Page County Heritage Association and was moved to the town of Luray in 1974.

participate. Only by teaching effective, non-violent skills for conflict resolution can the trend of violence be curbed.

For many reasons, the school setting now plays a larger role in the lives of students. For many students, the school has become a surrogate parent. School districts now offer Head Start programs, preschool classes, school breakfasts, and latch-key sessions. Programs are also offered on self-protection, drug abuse, self-esteem, teen pregnancy, hygiene, and coping in families with divorce (OEA Reform 1).

Mentoring programs for at-risk students have been developed. Members of the community are involved in a one-to-one relationship with students. As role models, specially-trained adults provide encouragement and support for students who might otherwise have academic or discipline problems in school.

In the days of one-room schools and small communities, parent-teacher conferences were not even necessary. Parents supported the efforts of the teacher, and they frequently attended school events with their children. If there was a problem at school, it was quickly remedied. Homework was rarely given because of chores on the farm.

Today, communication between home and school requires more initiative. At home, children need more reassurance that their school work is an important duty, as they cope with many distractions. Because of television, children are often passive, and they expect to be constantly entertained. The lack of instant gratification in some tasks discourages them. In addition to parent-

Victorsville School is located on the public school campus in Blissfield, Michigan. Built in 1870 and last used in the mid-1960s, the school was moved from Ogden Township to its present location.

Chestnut Ridge School, District No. 6, Walnut Creek Township, Holmes County, Ohio.

teacher conferences, parenting classes and parent information programs are now a necessary part of the education process. In reality, parents are considered a child's first and foremost teacher.

Because of far-reaching changes in society, school discipline today is a major focus. Without effective discipline, schools cannot provide optimum learning situations. The goal of discipline now is not humiliation, but it is a means of reducing disruptive behavior. Schools must provide opportunities for students to learn more positive ways of relating to each other.

Basic classroom rules have not changed all that much. Working and playing well with others, handing in assignments on time, following directions, and not disturbing others are still goals of the classroom environment. Verbal warnings, loss of privileges such as recess, and after-school detentions can still be the punishment for infractions. However, school officials must also deal with greater problems of disruption.

There are many benefits which result from parental support in the education of children. Giving a child regular medical checkups, immunizations, and a balanced diet help his physical well-being. By reading to preschool children, parents can support an early interest in reading. Continuing daily reading habits and telling stories encourage the pattern. Limiting their television viewing to less than two hours a day can challenge kids toward more creative outlets for their time and energy. Applying math and science to everyday situations helps a child understand their usefulness.

Providing a regular, quiet place for homework, insisting on its completion, and reviewing papers together can help a child evaluate his progress. Parents can support school efforts to develop and maintain good behavior rather than placing blame on other classmates. By finding out important dates, parents can participate in school events and programs. They can also volunteer for committees and for tutoring at the school. Most of all, parents can build their child's confidence by giving positive feedback about his skills and abilities.

Schools and communities can reinforce the efforts of families to help meet children's basic needs. For children to be successful, all sectors of society must work together to improve social, health, and educational services available to families.

The first school on the upper Mississippi River was held at Fort Snelling in the 1820s. The limestone structure, which also served as a church, educated both children and enlisted men. During the Civil War, the school's size was doubled. The original school was torn down in 1878. The reconstructed fort in St. Paul represents the wilderness outpost and is Minnesota's first National Historic Landmark.

The gray limestone Mattocks School, built in 1871 for $1,800, has twenty-inch thick walls. First known as Webster School No. 8, the school was moved to the grounds of Highland Park High School, St. Paul, Minnesota, in 1964. Its unique feature is the continuous blackboard surrounding the room. Currently, the school houses a classroom for special education.

Chapter 15

As students progressed in knowledge,
The bell's heart swelled with pride,
Each graduate was well prepared
To face life's work in stride.

Majorie Weber

School Reform

Outside Influences Prompt Changes

Through the years, particularly after consolidation of schools removed local control, public schools have been affected by wider political events. Shortly after consolidation reforms, the Russians launched the Sputnik satellite into space. The launch represented Russia's advanced intellect and education. Our country's leaders interpreted the launch as a wake-up call that the United States did not rank first in scientific achievements. As a result, school reformers called for greater emphasis on advanced math and science coursework in public schools. In response, President Eisenhower proposed the National Defense Act of 1958 which was passed by Congress. With these curriculum changes, the federal government involved itself more directly with the public schools.

Schools do not exist isolated from changes in society. Throughout history, schools have been the vehicles for training future citizens to participate in the political and economic system. Many forces outside education try to steer changes to meet their needs and inter-

ests. School reform and whether or not public schools are doing their job are issues of public discourse. The world today is changing fast, and the need for an educated and skilled work force is a concern of officials in government and industry. Changes in schools are imminent.

Kismaric and Hieferman say parents first demanded school expansion due to the Baby Boom generation which ballooned after World War II. From 1950 to 1970, elementary school enrollment increased by two-thirds, and the federal government, along with new taxes and bond issues, struggled to keep up (30). The nuclear family units moved into sprawling suburbs and began to accumulate material goods. Parents read advice from Dr. Benjamin Spock about the steps of child rearing. As people experimented with this new life style, they took comfort in the uniformity of following the accepted norms. Families were portrayed on television as interacting happily in prescribed roles (Kismaric and Heiferman 64).

Reflecting these set roles of perfect behavior in idealized families were new

See kitty play with the book.
Kitty likes to play.
Kitty is a pretty kitty.
Can Ruth catch kitty?

Main characters in the Scott, Foresman, and Company reading series from the 1930s to the 1960s are familiar to millions of American adults today. The characters include from left: Tim, Puff, Spot, Sally, Jane, and Dick.

school textbooks such as the Dick and Jane series published by Scott, Foresman, and Company. These primary reading texts, which first appeared as early as 1930, were read by eighty percent of U.S. children in the 1950s. As Americans moved from the country to urban areas and the schools absorbed large numbers of immigrants, a systematic reading series which helped Americanize young schoolchildren was desired. According to Martha Slud, the Dick and Jane series, along with its supplemental reading materials such as word cards, charts, and workbooks, entranced and educated children from the 1930s to the 1960s.

The earlier, widely-used *McGuffey Readers*, first introduced in 1836, had stressed moral and religious lessons. Though graded in difficulty, they emphasized reading aloud and memorizing. Beginning readers struggled to comprehend the difficult vocabulary and concepts. In contrast, the Dick and Jane series contained colorful pictures depicting the carefree and secure lives of happy, well-behaved children who experienced fun adventures.

The idealized life in textbooks of the 1950s could not prevent the social issue of Civil Rights from affecting urban schools. Up until the 1950s, seventeen states and Washington, D.C., had allowed segregation of races in their public schools. In 1954, while Thurgood Marshall, the first black member of the U.S. Supreme Court, served as a justice, the Supreme Court banned racial segregation in public schools. This effort to change racial problems in society through the schools continued into the 1960s and 1970s with enforced bussing of black students to previously white schools.

With the passage of the Elementary and Secondary Education Act of 1965, the federal government expanded its financial role in public schools. This law provided federal aid to schools with impoverished children by establishing

such programs at Title I and Head Start. Today, the federal government provides $7 billion per year for Title I and has expanded Head Start to a year-long program which has assisted sixteen million children. In 1994, Early Head Start was initiated to provide intervention for impoverished children who were younger than four years old.

By 1975, the federal government was mandating that public schools educate all disabled children. Special education programs were begun for children with various handicaps. Then, in 1979, the federal government increased its visible role in education by creating the U.S. Department of

A wooden case on the wall protected these early maps and charts. When needed, the teacher could open the box and roll them down. Such classroom supplies were in use by the early 1900s.

The "Little White School House" in Ripon, Wisconsin, has the distinction of being the birthplace of the Republican Party. This political event occurred at a public meeting on March 20, 1854. A larger brick school replaced it, and for a time it became a home. A mobile voting booth is pictured to the right.

Education as a cabinet office under President Jimmy Carter.

In 1980, Republican President Ronald Reagan wanted to reduce the national government's direct role in telling schools what to do. Despite this, the National Commission on Excellence in Education issued a report on public schools in 1983 called "Nation at Risk." This report concluded that, even though we spend $215 billion annually on education, America is losing out to our economic competition such as Japan because of low standards and lack of purpose in our schools (Merrow Report).

The National Education Summit in Charlottesville, Virginia, organized in 1989 by President George Bush, was attended by state governors. Together, they proposed eight goals for schools to achieve by the year 2000. President Bush stated that the key for solving problems in schools is at the state and local levels.

Partnerships between schools and businesses can help use joint resources to support the teaching of science and math. Both teachers and students can take part in summer internships and on-site visits and tours to transfer learned lessons to the classroom. This increased communication between schools and businesses would better prepare students with the skills desired by businesses and industry and help students adapt to new technology, methods of work, and the job market.

Schools typically provide career exploration activities as early as middle school. Using the inquiry approach, there could be more rigorous course offerings in mathematics and science and also in computers and technology. High school juniors and seniors can participate in work-based learning opportunities to get first-hand experience about the daily demands and skills needed for certain jobs.

All facets of society must make education one of the top priorities. Too many students are still dropping out of school, especially in urban areas. The goals today must be to produce independent and productive citizens who can demonstrate and apply knowledge. They must pursue continuous learning and have flexible job skills. Because of worldwide interactions, students must possess a global perspective and recognize cultural differences.

General suggestions for school reforms typically include these areas:

1. National Standards of Achievement
2. Continuing Teacher Education

Clark School, a small frame building, has been moved to Riverside Park in Berlin, Wisconsin. The school is open occasionally in the summer months as a museum.

The Gibbs School, built in 1873 and still on its original site outside St. Paul, Minnesota, was started by Heman Gibbs who settled the wilderness area in 1849. Restrooms, a furnace, and a new entry room were added as a WPA project in the 1930s. Closed in 1959, the school is now owned by the University of Minnesota.

3. School-Based Management
4. Longer School Day/Year
5. Changes in Educational Funding
6. Expansion of Computer Use
7. Broader School Choice/Alternative Schools

Some trends, such as charter schools, free from public regulations, are one effort to provide unique educational settings. Quick fixes, such as school choice, vouchers, privatization, and home schooling, do not bring educational gains to everyone nor do they provide for economic reform in more equal funding for public education.

Reform should involve those who have a vested interest in education including parents, social agencies, and the business community. Educational accountability is the shared responsibility of the community and all levels of government. They share responsibility with school boards, teachers, and parents to encourage students to become active, life-long learners. No one group can do it without the help of the others. Together, we must all continue to seek creative ways to educate our children and help them cope.

Children today do not get the close, supportive family and community structure that existed in the days of one-room schools. While we can never return to those simpler times, the basic needs of children have not changed. And local input and support are still greatly needed.

One guideline for change is that small schools offer more benefits. Smaller student bodies cost no more to operate than large, impersonal ones. Small-sized schools provide a family atmosphere where children receive personal attention to positively build their individual strengths. Some practices, as old as the one-room school, can be recalled. These include the beliefs that everyone can learn, parents and teachers are partners, everyone should show respect for others, work should be completed on time, material can be mastered, and no one should advance who is not ready.

Teaching children is still the most significant task of American society. Through education, the past is remembered, the present is made meaningful, and the future is shaped. America's forefathers established public education in order to teach children the social skills and values of American life. The responsibility for providing schools was assigned to state governments. Public education, or quality education free to all children, has survived over the decades. The United States has the

The ca1840 Copenhagen School originally stood in southwest Naperville, Illinois. Reconstructed in 1982, the simple white structure exemplifies life during the 1800s at Naper Settlement, a historical museum.

oldest and most successful system of public education in the world. Schools have been the chief reason that the melting pot of American immigrants have had the opportunity to succeed. America has become a world leader today because of the tradition of free education available to everyone.

Even though economic and social issues have increased the public's concern about schools, the value and the belief in public education remains strong.

Thomas Jefferson said:

I know of no safe depository of the ultimate powers of society but the people themselves. If we think them not enlightened enough to exercise their control with wholesome discretion, the remedy is not to remove them, but to inform their discretion by education.

Rural Hall School, District No. 8, 1908, Pulaski Township, Williams County, Ohio, with teacher Mabel Hubbell.

Chronology

1647 - Court of Massachusetts suggests building one-room schools.

1779 - Thomas Jefferson presents Virginia "Bill for the more General Diffusion of Knowledge," the forerunner of free public schools.

1785 - Federal Land Act measures the land west of Appalachian Mountains.

1787 - Northwest Ordinance opens territory for settlements.

1802 - Ohioans write a state constitution.

1803 - Ohio becomes first state carved from the Northwest Territory.

1820 - Surveyors lay out Williams County in Ohio's northwest corner.

1825 - First Ohio law establishes free public education for all.

1836 - William McGuffey first introduces his readers and spellers.

1837 - Settlers build Williams County's first log school in St. Joseph Township.

1838 - Ohio establishes system of county school superintendents and township inspectors.

1847 - Ohio's "Akron Laws" set up school system with eight grades.

1849 - Ohio passes school attendance law which says that students from ages eight to fourteen must go to school for twelve weeks.

1853 - Ohio sets two-mill tax levy to fund schools.

1870 - Individual manufactured desks replace homemade school desks.

1880 - Ohio makes laws which require teacher certification.

1890s - Brick schoolhouses become more common.

1890 - Kerosene lamps gain wide use in schools.

1892 - Ohio officials administer first eighth-grade exams.

1894 - Teachers present Palmer method of handwriting to students.

1900s - State of Ohio requires teachers to attend State Normal Schools.

1903 - Speech at National Education Association Convention favors school consolidations.

1917 - Consolidation becomes an issue in Williams County.

1920 - More Americans live in towns than in the country.

1921 - "Bing Laws" extend school year to 180 days or thirty-six weeks.

1930s - Electricity arrives in one-room schools.

1930 - Scott, Foresman first publishes its "Dick and Jane" reading series for primary students.

1940 - Ohio State Legislature outlines procedures for consolidating schools.

1944 - Ohio establishes State Board of Education.

1957 - Williams County completes consolidation of its schools.

1960s - Laws mandate that new teachers get four-year college degrees instead of two-year Normal degrees.

1965 - Federal government passes Elementary and Secondary Education Act.

1972 - Amish win the right to educate their children through the eighth grade in separate schools.

1975 - Federal government passes law to educate all handicapped children in public schools.

1979 - Federal government establishes U.S. Department of Education and Cabinet post.

1989 - Governors from all fifty states meet to write National Education Goals for the Year 2000.

1990s - Ohio State Department of Education develops State Proficiency Tests to include grades four, six, nine, and twelve.

1991 - Ohio Coalition for Equity and Adequacy of School Funding files suit in Perry County on behalf of school districts in Ohio.

1997 - Ohio Supreme Court rules that state's method of funding schools is unconstitutional and gives lawmakers one year to create new funding mechanism.

2000 - State of Ohio sets new minimum academic requirements for graduation from Ohio's schools.

Activities for Visiting A On-Room School

Plan a group visit to a restored one-room schoolhouse to experience early education and do the following:

1. Read beforehand from selected books about the history of one-room schools.

2. Interview former one-room school teachers and students.

3. Pre-plan details prior to the school visit, such as how to dress and what lunch items to take. Discuss what lessons will be like.

4. During the actual visit, carry out a typical schedule and lessons in the style of a one-room school classroom.

5. After the visit, compare one-room school activities to practices in present-day classrooms.

Ideas for Dress

Boys	Girls
Long, loose-fitting trousers (rolled up)	Knee-length cotton dress
Long socks pulled up over pants	Apron
Blousey-style cotton shirt	Bonnet
Suspenders	Long stockings
Ribbon tie at neck	Hair ribbon
Cap	Dark and sturdy shoes
Dark and sturdy shoes	

Suggested Lunch Items

Boys and girls should carry their lunch in a basket, cloth bundle, or in a round, tin lunch bucket. Possible menu items are:

Meats: Chicken, ham, sausage, bacon, beef jerky, eggs, cheese

Fruits and Vegetables: Tomatoes, corn on the cob, potatoes, apples, applesauce, pears, grapes, berries, pickles

Bread: Biscuits, cornbread, homemade bread, Johnny cake

Desserts: Fruit pie, honey cakes, ginger bread, oatmeal cookies, cake

Other: Popcorn, pumpkin seeds, nuts, jelly

Drinks: Tomato juice, apple juice, homemade root beer, water (in a glass jar)

Possible Daily Schedule

9:00	Teacher rings bell
9:05	Opening Exercises and Job Assignments
9:15	Reading and Penmanship
9:45	Arithmetic
10:15	Morning Recess
10:30	Elocution
11:00	Lunch and Games
12:00	Story
12:15	Geography and History
12:45	Science
1:15	Spelling
1:45	Jobs and Dismissal

Lessons

Morning Exercises

After the teacher rings the bell, students line up outside, boys on the left and girls on the right. Each line may file into the room separately. After children enter, they may hang their coats on wooden wall pegs and place their lunches on the shelves in the back of the room.

Boys may sit in seats on the left side of the classroom and girls may sit on the right side of the room. Students can be divided into eight grade levels. Students representing the primary grades should sit in the small desks near the front, while older students sit toward the back.

Opening exercises include the Pledge of Allegiance followed by a patriotic song. The teacher may also read a Bible verse. Assignments are already written on the blackboard for each grade level. Materials should be passed out including slates, erasers, pencils, copybooks, and readers.

Jobs

The teacher should assign classroom jobs to be done during the day. These could include filling the coal bucket or woodbox, filling the water pail, cleaning the blackboard, cleaning the erasers, dusting, sweeping the floor, and distributing and collecting materials.

Reading

Reading can be taught using pages from *McGuffey Readers*. Each group comes forward to the recitation bench by grade level. Typically, the teacher introduces the vocabulary words from the assigned story. Next, students read the story silently, then, in unison, and finally, aloud individually. Questions at the end of the story can be answered orally. (This process usually required more than one day.)

Penmanship

Students can write on their slates or in copybooks using quill pens and ink dipped from an inkwell. (Ink was typically made from ink powder mixed with water or from the boiled bark of a maple tree.) Students should practice forming the shape of letters as well as copying sayings.

Arithmetic

Old arithmetic books taught basic computation of number facts from one through twelve, along with fractions and percentages. Often, rhymes were recited as students memorized facts. Students can be drilled in basic facts by doing ciphering races on slates or at the board.

When texts were unavailable, teachers created their own story problems from the everyday lives of students. Sometimes, information for problems was borrowed from the Sears and Roebuck catalog.

Elocution

Correct pronunciation of words was as important as learning to spell. Students can practice phrases with alliterations. An example is: A big black bug bit a big black bear and the big black bear bled blood. Popular poems such as "The Village Blacksmith" by Henry W. Longfellow could be recited.

Geography and History

Since history of the United States was emphasized the most, students could practice writing the states and their capitals. They could memorize the names of lakes, rivers, and mountains. They can also memorize some dates which were important in our country's development such as 1492, 1776, 1812, and 1860-1865.

Or, invite a former one-room school teacher or student to come to speak to students about the days of one-room schools. Another idea is to have a resource person talk about the history of the schoolhouse being visited.

Science

Science might include focusing on nature near the schoolyard. Trees, plants, and insects can be identified. Students could collect and identify leaves. Students may write about changes in nature from season to season.

Spelling

Younger children may spell aloud words which are written on the blackboard. It would be appropriate to hold a spelldown or spelling bee. Students can compete against each other individually or in teams. During a spelling bee, each child is asked to spell a word. If the word is spelled incorrectly, the child has to sit down. The winner is the last person standing.

Words related to school and various subjects could be used. Examples would be slate, stove, blackboard, bench, inkwell, ruler, quill, bucket, rules, teacher, recess, spelldown, recite, penmanship, chalk, drill, reading, arithmetic, and geography. Other spelling words could be related to pioneer life.

Outdoor Games

Blind Man's Bluff

A handkerchief is tied over the eyes of one person. Players form a circle with the blindfolded person in the center. Players make noises and move around. The blindfolded person tries to catch one of the other players. The player he catches then becomes "it" and is blindfolded.

Drop the Handkerchief

Players stand in a circle and join hands. One player walks around the outside of the circle and drops a handkerchief behind another player. That player picks up the handkerchief, and then runs around the circle in the opposite direction trying to beat the one who dropped it back to his spot.

Red Rover

Two teams each form a line opposite each other while standing about fifteen to twenty feet apart. Team members hold hands, and they take turns calling out the name of someone on the opposite team. The chant is, "Red Rover, Red Rover, send (name of child) right over." That person runs over and attempts to break through the line. If he can't break through, he must join that team. If he does succeed in breaking the line, he chooses someone to take back to his team.

Crack the Whip

Everyone forms a line by holding the hand of the person in front of him and the person behind him. The leader runs and then suddenly makes a sharp turn. The goal is for those at the end of the line to hang on during the sudden twists and turns.

Ante, Ante, Over the Shanty

The ante is a ball, and the shanty is the school. Students are divided into two teams, and they stand on opposite sides of the schoolhouse. Someone from one team tosses the ball over the building and yells "Ante, ante, over the shanty." When someone on the opposite side catches the ball, both teams run around the schoolhouse counterclockwise and trade places. When the person carrying the ball reaches the other side, he tries to hit members of the opposing team who may still be there. If hit, that person must join the other team.

Other Outdoor Games

Other outdoor games besides playing with marbles or horseshoes and jumping rope are Fox and Geese, Corner Ball, Dodge Ball, Farmer in the Dell, Tug of War, and King of the Hill.

Indoor Games

Button, Button, Who's Got the Button?

Players form a circle with one person in the center. Players in the circle pass the button inconspicuously by hand from one person to the next. The person in the center has to guess who has the button. If he guesses right, the person who had the button goes into the center, and the one who had been in the center becomes part of the circle.

Hide the Thimble

Send a child out of the room while another child hides a thimble somewhere in the classroom. When the first child returns, he must hunt for the thimble. Other children can give hints by saying "hot" or "cold" when the child is near or far away from the hidden thimble. When the child finds the thimble, he sends someone else out while he hides the thimble again.

Other Indoor Games

Other possible indoor games are Gossip and Upset the Fruit Basket.

REPRODUCTION OF THE EARLY AMERICAN HORNBOOK

References

"Annual Report 1995-96, Bryan City Schools." *Bear Prints*, Nov. 1996: 5.

Apps, Jerry. *One Room Country Schools, History and Recollections from Wisconsin* (Amherst, Wis.: Amherst Press, 1996).

Cooley, Richard. "How the Old Country Schools Were Named." *Northwest Historian*, Sept. 1991: 4.

Cooley, Richard, and Kevin Maynard. *A Guide to Williams County History* (Montpelier, Ohio: Williams Co. Historical Soc., 1995).

Cummins, H.J. "First Lady's Here." *Star Tribune* (Minneapolis, Minn.) Mar. 1, 1996, late ed., sec. A: 1+.

Fuller, Wayne E. *One-Room Schools of the Middle West* (Lawrence, Kans.: UP of Kansas, 1994).

Geesey, Grace Zeiter. Personal Interview, July 23, 1996.

Good, Howard E. *Black Swamp Farm* (Columbus, Ohio: Ohio State UP, 1967).

Goodspeed, Weston, and Charles Blanchard, Ed. *History of Williams County, Ohio, Historical and Biographical* (Chicago, Ill.: F.A. Battery and Co., Pub., 1882).

Gulliford, Andrew. *America's Country Schools* (Washington, D.C.: Preservation Press, 1984).

Henry, Tamara. "One-Room Schools Aren't History," *USA Today*, April 7, 1997, sec. Life.

Highway Map: Williams County Ohio 1997 (Map Works, Inc., 1996).

"In Schools We Trust," Merrow Report, PBS. WBGU, Bowling Green, Ohio, Jan. 10, 1997.

Kalman, Bobbie. *Historic Communities: A One-Room School* (New York, N.Y.: Crabtree Pub. Co., 1994).

Kismaric, Carol, and Marvin Heiferman. *Growing Up with Dick and Jane* (San Francisco, Calif.: Collins, 1996).

Klimuska, Edward S. *Amish One-Room Schools: Lessons for the Plain Life* (Lancaster, Pa.: Lancaster Newspaper Services, 1992).

Kline, John B., Ed. *Country Schools and Their Recess Games* (Denver, Pa.: Saul Printing, 1990).

Kopf, Amy. "Disorders Are Growing Concerns." *Defiance Crescent News*, May 25, 1997, Sec. A: 1+.

Lapp, Christ S. *Pennsylvania School History 1690-1990* (Elverson, Pa.: Mennonite Family History, 1991).

"Legislative Update: How the New Licensure Legislation Will Affect You," *Ohio Schools*, Sept. 1996: 6-7.

Lieberman, Myron. *Public Education: An Autopsy* (Cambridge, Mass.: Harvard UP, 1993).

Merrow Report. See "In Schools We Trust."

Norton, Ruth M. *A Fine Poor Man's Country: The Life of Ohio's Early Craftsmen* (Coshocton, Ohio: Roscoe Village Foundation, 1991).

OEA Reform. See *Ohio Education Reform Package*.

OEA Task Force. "Report of the Ideal Classroom Task Force of the Ohio Education Association" (Columbus, Ohio: Ohio Education Association, 1990).

Ohio Education Reform Package. Adopted by OEA Representative Assembly (Columbus, Ohio: Ohio Education Association, 1993).

Rosevink, Richard, Chm. *History of Defiance County, Ohio, Illustrated* (Defiance, Ohio: Defiance Co. Historical Soc., 1976).

Sabo, Sandra R. "Shaping School Design." *Northwest Ohio SERRC* (Winter Quarterly 1996: 12-15).

Schinn, William Henry. *History of William County, Ohio* (Madison, __: Northwest Historical Assoc., 1905).

Sheeley, Mary L., Ed. *Putnam County, Ohio, One-Room Schools* (Kalida, Ohio: Putnam Co. Historical Soc., 1985).

Slud, Martha. "Dick, Jane, and Spot to be Recalled by Baby Boomers." *Bryan Times*, Mar. 11, 1994: 13.

Stewart, Dr. J. Mark, Sr., Consult. *Ohio: Adventures in Time and Place* (New York, N.Y.: Macmillan McGraw-Hill, 1996).

Thomas, Mary Hutchinson. *Sesquicentennial of Education on Millcreek West Unity Schools 1834-1984*. (Williams Co., Ohio: n.p., [1984]).

U.S. Census. "What the U.S. Census Tells Us About Children." Center for the Study of Social Policy [1990].

Voinovich, Gov. George. *Destination: Success In Education, Journey to the Year 2000*. Ohio's Fifth Annual Goals Progress Report, Columbus, Ohio: [State Dept. of Education, 1995].

Wagner, Chloe C. *Ohio: A Profile* (Cincinnati, Ohio: Ohio Teaching Aids, 1983).

"WCHS Voters to Aid County Commissioners." *Northwest Historian*, Jan. 1992: 1.

Webb, Michele, Ed. *My Folks and the One-Room Schoolhouse* (Topeka, Kans.: Capper Press, 1993).

Index